As a Child

# As a Child
## God's Call to Littleness

Phil Steer

lulu.com

Copyright © 2012 Phil Steer

First published 2012 by lulu.com

Phil Steer has asserted his moral right to be identified as the author of this work.

All rights reserved. No part of this publication may be reproduced, stored in a retrieval system, or transmitted in any form or by any means without the prior written permission of the copyright owner.

asachildbook.com
facebook.com/asachildbook
twitter @asachildbook

Scripture taken from the Holy Bible, NEW INTERNATIONAL VERSION®. Copyright © 1973, 1978, 1984 by Biblica, Inc. All rights reserved worldwide. Used by permission.

Cover photograph © Joanna Zielinska / Fotolia

Design advice from www.thebookdesigner.com

ISBN 978-1-4476-7531-0

*To my Mum and Dad
For my childhood,
And my wife, Ali,
And my children,
Josh, Tom & Rebecca.*

At that time the disciples came to Jesus and asked, "Who is the greatest in the kingdom of heaven?"

He called a little child and had him stand among them. And he said: "I tell you the truth, unless you change and become like little children, you will never enter the kingdom of heaven. Therefore, whoever humbles himself like this child is the greatest in the kingdom of heaven. And whoever welcomes a little child like this in my name welcomes me."

Matthew 18:1–5

# Contents

| | |
|---|---|
| *Acknowledgements* | xi |
| *As a Child* | 1 |
| Preface | 3 |
| Greatest | 7 |
| Child | 13 |
| Childish | 17 |
| Welcomes | 23 |
| Change | 29 |
| Humbles | 33 |
| Enter | 39 |
| Believed | 45 |
| Revealed | 51 |
| Receive | 59 |
| Belongs | 65 |
| Called | 71 |
| Obedient | 77 |
| Discipline | 83 |
| Pray | 89 |
| Praise | 95 |
| Hinder | 101 |
| Blessed | 107 |
| Become | 113 |
| References | 121 |

# Acknowledgements

I never envisaged that I'd write a book. Without the help and encouragement of many others I would not have started, let alone completed, *As a Child*. Here I offer my grateful thanks.

To Ray Sammé, former vicar of The Church of the Good Shepherd, Collier Row, Romford, for encouraging me to preach and for giving me so many opportunities to do so. Preparing for these talks was invaluable experience in learning how to explore ideas and express them in writing.

To Nick Hyde, without whose unexpected enquiry I would never have thought of writing this book.

To Paul Wallis, for our many years of friendship and for his great encouragement to me in writing *As a Child*, especially during the crucial early stages.

To my wife, Ali, and my children, Josh, Tom & Rebecca, for all the childlike times we've shared, and for the times we missed when I was "writing my book".

To Russell Pilkington, for his astute observation on page 80.

To all who took the time to consider a draft manuscript and who provided me with encouragement, comments and suggestions: Ken Ashton, Johnny Douglas, Nigel Dutson, Mark Earey, Phil Grundy, David Hague, Anne Howson, Michaela Hyde, Nick Hyde, Chris James, Russell Pilkington and Andy Poultney. The book is certainly better for their input; the faults that remain are, of course, mine alone.

To Tim Garwood, for enhancing the cover photograph.

And last but not least my thanks to you, for obtaining a copy of this book and for taking the time to read it. I hope and pray that you find it worthwhile.

# As a Child

As a child I found delight in leaf and twig and tree.
Such simple gifts of nature were a source of joy to me.
Birds singing in the tree-tops, the sun against my face,
Splashing through the puddles, as round the woods I'd race.

Taking home a sticky-bud and placing in a jar,
Then watching slowly open the green five-pointed star.
Collecting burnished conkers, lying where they fell,
Amongst the Autumn-tinted leaves and peeping from the shell.

But now it seems much harder to enjoy such simple things;
To receive with open hands and heart the gifts that each day brings.
No longer just accepted with unconsidered pleasure,
But analysed and categorised, I miss the hidden treasure.

O to be a child again! And put off grown up ways.
To know again the myriad gifts with which you fill my days.
To know you as my Father, and to know that I'm your son,
And as a child to trust your ways until my days are done.

# Preface

Early in January 2000 I went on a retreat day with a group from the church that I belong to. The day was not led or structured in any way, but simply provided some time and space for quiet reflection at the start of the new millennium. I decided that I'd not make any particular attempt to hear God through Bible reading or prayer, but rather take advantage of this rare opportunity simply to just "be". I wandered around the grounds for a while, and then stopped alongside a small patch of land. There was, to be honest, nothing especially notable or attractive about the place. I seem to recall that it was more scrub than anything else, with a few trees and bushes and long grass and perhaps a small pond. But there I stopped and stood, and looked and listened, and tried simply to drink in the scene before me.

I should say this is not something that comes easily. I am not good at paying attention to all that is around me. I live perhaps too much of my life inside my head: so caught up in my thoughts that I miss the world outside – the world of the senses – seldom truly seeing or feeling or smelling or touching or tasting. But this was one of those rare occasions. As I fixed my gaze on the scene before me and attuned my ears to the sounds around me, so my mind became stilled in the stillness, and I became more and more present in that moment and in that place.

After a while the words of a poem began to form in my mind, and by the end of the day I had completed "As a Child". Now I am not going to pretend that these are the greatest lines ever penned, but they do nonetheless capture the essence of what I was thinking and feeling at that time. Perhaps more importantly, they also capture something of what I believe to have been God's word for me that day: the need for a more childlike approach to my life and faith.

A couple of years later I was asked to give a talk at church on the subject of "Life in the Kingdom", looking at the events recounted in Matthew chapter 18. As I prepared the talk I found myself increasingly drawn to the first five verses of the passage, where Jesus speaks of the need for us to become like little children. I felt strongly this was an important and profound message that I had largely missed up until then. I could not recall it featuring too often in talks I had heard or in books I had read. Certainly I had barely begun to take on board the implications of Jesus' words for my own life and faith.

I concluded the talk with the poem that I'd written on that retreat day a couple of years earlier. I remarked that it seemed that God had been speaking to me then about the need to become more childlike, and I wondered aloud whether I had paid proper attention to what he might have been saying.

I must confess, despite my strong sense of the importance of the message, in the years that followed I made little effort

## Preface

to pursue its implications or put these into practice in my life.

Then some years later, quite out of the blue, a friend asked me, "So, when will you be writing your book?" This was something I'd never seriously considered, and I immediately dismissed the idea. But later, pondering this unexpected enquiry, I remembered my talk – and it occurred to me that this was a subject that perhaps I might be able to explore further. At the very least, I would benefit from doing so: it would cause me to look again at Jesus' call to childlikeness, and so give his words another chance to begin truly to change and transform my life. This little book is the result.

The book is based around those words of Jesus from Matthew 18, along with other passages that relate particularly to the place of children in the kingdom of heaven, and their relationship with their heavenly Father. Each chapter focuses on a single word from one of these passages, and explores what that word, that concept, that idea, might mean in the context of this call to childlikeness. What might it mean, for example, to *humble* ourselves like a little child or *receive* like a little child or *pray* like a little child? What might it mean to *become* like a little child?

I should say up front that this book is more about what childlikeness might look like, rather than how it might be attained. As such, you may find yourself wishing for some practical suggestions at the end of each chapter; frustrated, even, that I hold up the goal of childlikeness, then seemingly won't tell you how to get there. But childlikeness is not something that can be attained simply by following some twelve step plan (an approach that appeals more to the adult we are than the child we seek to become). Rather, as Paul tells the church in Rome, we are to be transformed by the renewing of our minds.[1] If this book in any way changes your thinking about childlikeness — to see it as important and believe it worth pursuing — then it will have fulfilled all my hopes.

I know full well that I have scarcely scratched the surface, barely begun to plumb the depths of what this call to childlikeness might mean. And certainly I can not claim to live an especially childlike life. Yet I am more convinced than ever of the importance of us heeding Jesus' call: of the need for us to become like little children. I know, of course that this is not the whole picture: just one facet of our faith. Nonetheless, I truly believe that it is fundamental to us entering into all that God has for us, of living the life that he wants us to live, and of becoming the people that he wants us to be. I hope and pray that, having read this book, you too might feel encouraged to respond to this call to childlikeness, and to discover more and more of what it means for you to live your life "as a child".

# Greatest

At that time the disciples came to Jesus and asked, "Who is the **greatest** in the kingdom of heaven?"[1]

"Who is the greatest in the kingdom of heaven?" If someone were to come to you and ask this question, how would you reply? Forget for a moment the words of Jesus on the subject. What I am looking for here is not the "correct" theological answer, but rather your own instinctive response. Not, who does Jesus say that it is, but who do *you* say that it is? Who do you, in all honesty, consider to be the greatest in the kingdom of heaven? Or if not the greatest, who do you think of as being among the greatest? Who are the "best" Christians, those whom you look up to and admire, who encourage and inspire you, whose lives you aspire to?

Now it may be that one or two names spring readily to mind. But, on the other hand, you might reply that you really don't think in such terms; that you don't judge your fellow believers in this way; that there are no first-class and second-class Christians; that we are all equally loved by God. You might even quote Paul's first letter to the church in Corinth, where he speaks of the church as a body in which every part is equally necessary and equally honoured.[2] And it may well be that this is indeed what you believe. But I'd

## As a Child

tentatively suggest that this is probably not the whole story, because none of us can quite help ourselves from making such assessments of others. It is something that we do automatically, instinctively, unconsciously, whether we intend to or not.

It might be a church leader or a preacher or a teacher; a worship leader or an evangelist or an intercessor; someone of international renown or of national fame or of local standing or even a relative unknown; someone from the distant past or someone from the present; someone known to you personally or simply through their work and reputation.

Whoever the person might be, my guess is that for many of us it is likely to be someone whom we feel has "made a difference for God" in the world, in the church and in our lives. Perhaps this might be one of the Saints or "heroes" from Church history; or in today's celebrity culture, it might well be one of the "names" on the Christian celebrity circuit – those whose books we read, whose songs we sing, whose teachings we seek to follow.

Now it is not wrong to have other Christians as role-models. Indeed, Paul urged the Corinthian church to imitate him and his "way of life in Christ Jesus,"[3] whilst the writer of the book of Hebrews counselled his readers to remember their leaders, to consider the outcome of their way of life, and to imitate their faith.[4] It all depends, however, on whom those role-models are, and what it is about their lives that inspires us.

We need to ask ourselves whether our measure of greatness within the kingdom of heaven is really very different from the measure of greatness used in the world at large, concerned so often, as it is, with fame and fortune, accolades and achievements, position and prestige and power. Do we see greatness where God sees it, or are our heads turned by these worldly attractions?

This is why the question of who we consider to be "the greatest in the kingdom" is such a significant one: because our answer to it will reveal much about our values and the things that we think of as important and worthwhile. This, in turn, will affect the way in which we spend our time and our energy, our money and our resources – both as individual Christians and as a body of believers.

But just because this is how we measure greatness today, does it necessarily mean that the same was true in Biblical times? Is this what Jesus' disciples had in mind when they asked him, "who is the greatest in the kingdom of heaven"?

Certainly it seems not unreasonable to assume that the understanding of greatness in Biblical times was – to some extent, at least – not a million miles from our own. They even had a version of our celebrity culture. Just think of the rivalry between the first groups of Christians: between those who claimed to be followers of Paul, or of Apollos, or of Cephas, or of Christ.[5] Or think of the crowds that flocked to see John the Baptist and Jesus. Without doubt many came with a genuine hunger and desire to hear from God's messengers and to respond to his word spoken through them. Many others, however, will have come simply to see these men that the whole world seemed to be talking about, to be part of the "event", to be able to say, "I was there."

But the disciples' question went beyond such subjective assessments of greatness. In Matthew's account their enquiry appears to be of purely academic interest, born out of a desire to learn something more from Jesus about the workings of the kingdom. But read Luke's account and a very different picture emerges. For it turns out that the disciples have been

## As a Child

arguing – and it will probably come as little surprise to discover that their argument concerned which of *them* was the greatest. It went without saying, of course, that it had to be one of them: they were, after all, Jesus' closest disciples, the chosen Twelve, so they must be pretty special. But which of them was number one, the "first among equals", the greatest of them all?

This was not simply a question of them wanting Jesus to massage their egos, and make them feel good about themselves. It must be remembered that the disciples were still anticipating that Jesus would soon be ushering in his earthly kingdom. Indeed, even after he was raised from the dead, this expectation had not entirely disappeared – hence their asking the risen Jesus, "Lord, are you at this time going to restore the kingdom to Israel?"[6]

The disciples understood the nature of kingdoms far better than most of us do today. The lands in which they lived, worked and travelled were all provinces of the mighty Roman Empire, with the Emperor as supreme ruler and commander. They knew full well that the Emperor was unquestionably the greatest in the Empire, and that the greatness of others was largely determined by him. He could bestow greatness on any that he chose by awarding them positions of influence, authority and power; and he could cause them to fall from grace by withdrawing his favour. The greatest in the Empire were those closest to the Emperor, those with whom he chose to surround himself, his most trusted friends and advisers.

The disciples were confident that they were in Jesus' inner circle, and now they were asking which of them would be given the position of greatest honour in his coming kingdom. You can almost sense their expectancy as they await Jesus'

*Greatest*

answer. But his answer, when it came, could not have been further from what they hoped and expected to hear.

# Child

He called a little **child** and had him stand among them.[1]

The disciples have just asked Jesus, "Who is the greatest in the kingdom of heaven?" (or, more to the point, which of them is the greatest in the kingdom of heaven) and now they await his reply. There is, perhaps, just a hint of tension in the air, an uneasy truce at the end of all their squabbling. Soon they will have their answer; the argument will be settled once and for all. Some have reason to be quietly confident: Simon Peter, the "rock" on whom Jesus would build his church;[2] James and John, the brothers who, with Peter, were granted a "mountain-top experience", seeing Jesus transfigured and speaking with Moses and Elijah.[3] Others realise that they are probably not the front-runners, but still feel that they are in with a chance: Andrew, Simon Peter's brother, who was the first to follow Jesus;[4] Nathaniel, whom Jesus called "a true Israelite";[5] Judas, who has been entrusted with their money.[6] The rest of the group wait more in hope than expectation; Thomas, especially, has his doubts.

There is, perhaps, a pause whilst Jesus appears to consider his reply, only adding to the tension and sense of anticipation. And then he calls forward a little child. Seemingly, Jesus

## As a Child

hasn't heard their question. Or maybe he has chosen to ignore it? That would be just like him! So often in the past he has failed to give a straight answer to a perfectly straightforward question. Should they try asking again? And then Jesus speaks: "Unless you change and become like little children, you will never enter the kingdom of heaven." What was that? "Never enter the kingdom of heaven"? Had they heard him correctly? Far from confirming their belief that they were near the top – if not at the top – of the spiritual pile, Jesus seems to be bringing into question whether they are even in the kingdom at all. And what was all this about becoming like little children? What on earth did that mean? How could they become like little children? And why would they want to?

You can almost hear their heads spinning as they try to get to grips with what Jesus has just said, and see their exchanged glances as they wonder which of them will be the first to voice the thoughts that are racing through their minds. But before they have a chance to say anything, Jesus continues: "Therefore, whoever humbles himself like this child is the greatest in the kingdom of heaven."

What was this? The greatest in the kingdom of heaven was not Simon Peter or James or John, Jesus' closest companions; not another of the "chosen Twelve", who had left everything to follow him; not one of Jesus' many other followers; not even one of the Pharisees or Sadducees or teachers of the Law. No, the greatest in the kingdom of heaven was, apparently, anyone who humbled themselves like a little child.

By our usual criteria of greatness, this sounds like nonsense. How can a mere child possibly be great? Too young to have developed the abilities and skills and strengths that adults possess, what can a child possibly achieve? What position can they attain? What influence do they have? What

*Child*

authority can they be given? What power can they exercise? But all this is of no importance. A child is great in the kingdom of God for one reason above all others: because Jesus, the King of kings and Lord of lords, says that they are. Greatness in the kingdom is not something that can be attained through our own efforts and abilities, but rather something that is given by God. Just as the Roman Emperor could bestow greatness upon any that he chose to be part of his inner circle, so Jesus bestows greatness on those whom he calls closest to himself, on those who come to him like little children.

It is almost impossible for us to appreciate the full impact of Jesus' words on his disciples. We know full-well what he was going to say, and so there is not the utter shock and surprise that they would have experienced on hearing his answer for the first time. But perhaps more than this, we also miss something of the reality – I might say the physicality – of Jesus' words. The disciples were not asking an abstract, theological question. They were expecting Jesus to bring about God's kingdom on earth, to "restore the kingdom to Israel",[7] and they really wanted to know which of them would hold the positions of greatest honour and power. And Jesus didn't give them an abstract, theological answer. Rather, he called a forward little child – a real little child – and he said, if you want to be great in the kingdom of heaven then *be like this*.

There is, I think, a tendency for us to understand Jesus' words to be simply an illustration, a metaphor of the need to have a childlike faith and a childlike trust in God. But to limit their meaning in this way is, I believe, to diminish the all-embracing, life-changing scope of what Jesus is actually asking of us. For the call to be childlike is one that has signifi-

## As a Child

cance for each and every aspect of our daily lives.

Too many of us have lost touch with the child that we once were: left behind in our rush into the adult world, forgotten in our fascination with adult ways, banished for fear they might make us look foolish and neglected when it seemed they were no longer needed. Others, I know, will have been forced by circumstance to grow up far too quickly, never having the opportunity truly to live as the child that God created you to be. As a consequence we live our lives largely separated from our childlike self. But this is not the way we are meant to be. And so Jesus calls us to become like little children, to recover our childlike nature, and so discover the fullness of a kingdom that only the childlike can enter.

# Childish

When I was a child, I talked like a child, I thought like a child, I reasoned like a child. When I became a man, I put **childish** ways behind me.[1]

"Oh, grow up! Act your age! Stop being so childish!" What parents have not, at some time or other, uttered exclamations such as these in utter exasperation at their child's behaviour? We are generally fairly willing to indulge childish behaviour from the very young; indeed, we might even find it rather amusing and endearing. But as our children grow older and begin to learn how they ought to behave, we find it less and less acceptable when they don't do as they should – and quite right too!

The apostle Paul seems to echo these cries of the exasperated parent in his letters to the churches in Corinth and Ephesus: "put childish ways behind you", "stop thinking like children,"[2] "no longer be infants" and "grow up."[3] What could be clearer? Childhood is for children, not for adults. We are not meant to remain stuck in the patterns of thought and behaviour that characterised our early years. As we grow older we are to grow up, to develop, to mature. This is the way of things, the way that life should be.

When we think back to our children's early years, when we look at old photos and watch old home movies, we may perhaps sometimes experience a touch of nostalgic sadness. But the truth is that we wouldn't want them to stay that way for ever. For of course, there are some children who do not fully mature – be that physically, mentally, emotionally, or socially – and this can be a cause of great sadness.

But in calling for us to become like little children, Jesus is not saying that we should not grow and mature – and he is certainly not saying that we should continue in childish behaviour. His call is for us to become not child*ish* but child*like*, and there is a world of difference between the two. Indeed, sad to say, were it childish behaviour that Jesus seeks, there would be little need for him to encourage us in it, since this comes perfectly naturally to most of us.

It needs no special effort on my part to be immature, insecure, irresponsible and infantile – and I suspect that I am not alone in this. We can all be self-centred, attention-seeking and manipulative; we can all get angry and sulk if we don't get what we want. Being childish is not something that most of us lose as we grow up. We might become better at hiding such childish reactions, but that childish nature remains with us no matter how old we get.

Being childlike – as we shall see in the coming chapters – is something entirely different.

If we look at Paul's words in context we see that he is in no way discouraging childlike behaviour. His comment about putting childish ways behind him occurs towards the end of his teaching about love, famous for its use in countless wedding services. Prophecies will cease, tongues will be stilled, knowledge will pass away, but love will remain. When perfection comes, the imperfect disappears. Paul is cautioning a church that has become too preoccupied with the spiritual gifts. The gifts are important, but not that important. When compared with love, they are but childish things. Ultimately they will be left behind, as all childish things must be. When God's kingdom comes in all its fullness there will no longer be any need for spiritual gifts. They will pass, but love will remain.

Similarly, when Paul tells the church in Corinth to "stop thinking like children" he is again concerned with their attitude to spiritual gifts (and in particular the gift of tongues). They are not to be like a child with a new toy, playing with the gifts for their own pleasure and amusement. Rather, they are to exercise the gifts with wisdom and understanding, and to seek to grow in those gifts "that build up the church."[4] The gifts are given for the good of others, not to inflate our egos. Again, it is a childish attitude to the gifts — immature, self-centred and attention-seeking — that Paul is counselling against.

What then of Paul's instruction to the believers in Ephesus that they are to "grow up" and "no longer be infants"? This seems clear enough; but again, the context reveals a different story. The "infants" that Paul refers to are those whom he characterises as being "tossed back and forth by the waves, and blown here and there by every wind of teaching and by the cunning and craftiness of men in their deceitful scheming". In other words, to be an "infant" is to have an unsteady and uncertain faith, too easily drawn away from the truth of Christ by the lies of the world. It is being worldly, being immature in our faith, neither knowing nor living the truth of God's word. This is not the way we should be; instead, we are to grow up into Christ — into his truth, into his love, into the fullness of all that he is and all that he desires us to be.

"Put childish ways behind you", "stop thinking like children", "no longer be infants", "grow up". As we have seen, none of these statements from Paul in any way runs counter to Jesus' call for us to become more childlike. We are not to be immature in the level of our love, we are not to be immature in our use of the spiritual gifts, we are not to be immature in our understanding and practice of God's word. We are to grow out of such childish ways – but we are also to grow into the likeness of a child.

As I hope is clear, I am in no way suggesting that we should revert entirely to the attitudes and actions of childhood, rejecting all aspects of our adult life and faith. We should of course welcome and encourage the maturity, knowledge and experience that we gain as we grow into adulthood; for there are many situations and tasks and challenges that we need to approach as adults, drawing upon all the resources with which our years have endowed us.

When Jesus sent out the twelve disciples he counselled them to be "as shrewd as snakes and as innocent as doves."[5] He was, in effect, instructing them to combine the wisdom that comes from age and experience with the simplicity of a little child – an echo of his wider call for us to live undivided lives, our adult self and our childlike self journeying together, hand-in-hand, united as one.

We know just what it means to live as adults; it's what we do: naturally, instinctively, for the most part unthinkingly. Our adult self assumes his place as of right, whilst the little child is pushed to the margins. Hence, there is little need in the chapters that follow for me to keep putting the adult perspective, to give voice to the adult whom we know so well, and who all too often dismisses and drowns out the voice of the child. My purpose, therefore, is simply to do as Jesus did: to call forward our childlike self, to bring him out of obscurity, and to place her right in the centre of what it

*Childish*

means to live in the fullness of the kingdom of God.

# Welcomes

"And whoever **welcomes** a little child like this in my name welcomes me."[1]

For many of us the idea of welcome plays a key role in our understanding of how we relate to God. Seekers are exhorted to "welcome Jesus into their lives," new believers speak of "welcoming Jesus into their heart," those seeking to grow in the gifts are encouraged to "welcome the Holy Spirit". We think of "opening the door" to Jesus,[2] of God coming to make his home with us,[3] and of the need to let him into each and every area in our lives. And although at times we may wish that we could keep our life as our own, at heart we know that true life is to be found only when we are his.

And so we long for a closer relationship with God, long to welcome God the Father, God the Son, God the Holy Spirit – God in all his fullness. Yet in all our seeking and striving after God, how many of us learn from these words of Jesus, words that teach us how we might go about welcoming him into our lives? For whenever we welcome a little child as he would welcome a little child, then we welcome Jesus himself.

This is perhaps one of those passages that we have a tendency to skip over in our thinking. We find the words encouraging in a vague sort of way, yet do not stop to consider whether they might be anything more than metaphor. Is Jesus simply illustrating something of what it means to welcome him? Or is there some real sense in which, as we welcome a little child, so we also welcome the living Jesus into our lives? And, if that's the case, how might this be?

To begin with, in welcoming a little child we are simply doing as Jesus would do. He demonstrated his great love for little children, welcoming their presence and giving them a position of honour as the "greatest in the kingdom of heaven." Whenever we do the same, accepting his teaching and acting upon it, we ally ourselves with him and align our lives with his. In welcoming a child, we welcome the ways of God into our lives.

There is also the sense that, in welcoming a little child, we are welcoming one in whom God's divine nature is more fully present – or, at least, more clearly evident. The book of Genesis teaches that every person is made in the image of God. This is the root of our being, the essence of our nature, and it remains so in every person no matter how far from God they might stray. Hence, in every human encounter, we are in a very real sense encountering something of the reality of God. Whenever we welcome someone to share our home, our time, our life, so also welcome God. This is true of everyone, young or old; but it is especially true of a little child, where the divine nature has not yet become buried beneath the cares and concerns and trials and temptations of this world.

We can also find that in welcoming a little child we are welcoming one who comes as an emissary of Jesus. Just as a ruler or government will send someone to represent them and act on their behalf, so God sends little children to speak and act for him. In their simplicity and naivety they say and do things that we adults never would, but which can reveal deep truths about the way the world should be, if we only would have ears to hear and eyes to see ("out of the mouths of babes ..."[4] as the saying goes). God sends children to speak into our world, and by welcoming them, we welcome his word to us.

Since we welcome Jesus when we welcome a little child, so the way in which we welcome little children can teach us and train us in what in means to welcome Jesus. As we become more welcoming to little children, so this fosters within us the actions and attitudes of heart that enable us to be more welcoming to him.

To begin with, we recognise that little children could not care less about who we are in the eyes of the world. Title and status, accolades and achievements, position and power mean absolutely nothing. They do not relate to such external labels but rather to the person that we show ourselves to be in the ways in which we respond to them. And it goes without saying that the same is true of God. As he said to the prophet Samuel, "Man looks at the outward appearance, but the LORD looks at the heart."[5] Therefore, as we seek to welcome the person and work of God in our lives, we must set aside such worldly trappings: we must come instead just as we are, prepared to be seen just as we are, and willing to be met just as we are.

When we meet and speak with a little child we will often bend down or crouch down or get down on our knees – and with a baby we will even lie down flat on the floor. We do this in order to place ourselves at their level, to meet them where they are. We tend to think of kneeling or prostrating ourselves before God as being an act of submission and respect to the One who is immeasurably greater than we are – and this is right, of course. But perhaps there is also a sense in which we are bringing ourselves down to God's level; to the level of the One who has chosen to make himself small, who revealed himself as a helpless baby, and who even as a fully grown man constrained the fullness of his divinity within the limits of humanity. Just as the Magi bowed down to worship the infant Jesus,[6] so must we. When God makes himself small, we have little choice but to make ourselves smaller still.

Having recognised and responded to a little child, we then need to give them our time and our attention – not grudgingly or half-heartedly, with our mind elsewhere and our body eager to follow, but rather giving them the fullness of each moment and the totality of our attention. We need to watch closely and listen carefully in order to recognise and understand the child's needs and desires. We need to join with them in what they are doing, rather than expecting them to join in with us in what we are doing. And we need to be prepared for some mess and some noise, for some loss of control, and be willing to accept it rather than trying to prevent it – for a child's thoughts are not our thoughts, and neither are their ways our ways.[7] The parallels with what it means to welcome God into our lives are, I hope, clear to see.

All of this should be an encouragement for us as adults to seek to become more and more welcoming to little children, and through this to become more and more welcoming to Jesus. But of course, by far the best people to welcome little children are not adults at all – however child-friendly we might try to be – but rather other little children. They don't need to set aside the trappings of the world, because they have none; they don't need to make themselves small, because they already are; they don't need to try to relate to a child's way of being, because this comes completely naturally to them. In the same way, it is as a little child that we are best

*Welcomes*

able to welcome Jesus. And so, just as we need to learn to welcome little children as Jesus would do, so we need also to learn to welcome our own "inner-child". For the more childlike we become, the more welcoming we can be to the childlike Christ.

# Change

"I tell you the truth, unless you **change** and become like little children, you will never enter the kingdom of heaven."[1]

Are you one of those people who make New Year's resolutions? That moment, when the old year draws to a close and the new year stands open before us, can seem a particularly appropriate time to take stock of our lives, and resolve that things will be different from now on.

Many, feeling the effects of the Festive Season, resolve that they will lose weight and get fit: diet programmes are embarked upon; fitness equipment is purchased; health club membership soars. Others aim to improve their health by giving up smoking or by drinking less or by trying to reduce the stress in their lives. Some decide that they will improve their work and financial situation: by getting a better job or by saving some money or by paying off debts. Others want to expand their horizons by travelling or by learning something new; and still more resolve to spend more time with family and friends, and perhaps even find true love. For many the aim is simply to enjoy life more.

Whether or not we make New Year's resolutions, we all of us have a desire for change. Even the most contented will allow that their lives are not everything that they would want them to be – and most of us will surely accept that we are not the person that we want ourselves to be, nor the person that God wants us to be either. We know that we mess up and need to repent and receive forgiveness and allow ourselves to be transformed by God's Holy Spirit.

But how many of us have ever resolved that "this year, I will become more like a little child"? And how many of us, when we've allowed ourselves to acknowledge the fact that we're not the person we ought to be, have recognised that our biggest need might be to become more childlike? And yet this is exactly what Jesus is saying: we need to "change and become like little children."

Jesus underlines the importance of his message by introducing it with the words, "I tell you the truth". Whenever he uses this expression we know it is a sign that we really need to sit up and take note. What he is about to say is not simply true – after all, Jesus never spoke anything but the truth – but is a Truth, with a capital "T". It is something fundamental about the workings of the kingdom of heaven.

The word Jesus uses when he speaks of our need to change means "to turn around, to change direction". The implication is that if we are not becoming more and more childlike, then our lives are headed the wrong way. We might think that we are meant to grow up and become more adult; Jesus tells us that, on the contrary, we need in many ways to "grow down" and become more like little children. But what might this mean?

In his parable of the sower Jesus speaks of "the worries of this life, the deceitfulness of wealth and the desires for other things" that "come in and choke the word [that God sows in us], making it unfruitful."[2] Little children do not concern themselves with such things: such worries and deceitfulness

## Change

and desires. These, rather, are the attitudes and ambitions and anxieties of adulthood: "thorns" that grow up as we grow older, entangling our heart and mind, stifling our soul and spirit, and preventing us from entering into fullness of the kingdom of heaven.

In the same way, while some might debate the extent to which little children can be said to "sin", there can be little doubt that they succumb to very few of the temptations that so easily cause adults to stray from God's path and fall short of his standards. Writing to the churches in Galatia, Paul says, "The acts of the sinful nature are obvious: sexual immorality, impurity and debauchery; idolatry and witchcraft; hatred, discord, jealousy, fits of rage, selfish ambition, dissensions, factions and envy; drunkenness, orgies, and the like."[3] Look over that list again: little children just don't indulge in most of these things.

So Jesus' call for us to "change and become like little children" must surely have something to do with a turning away from sinful thoughts and words and deeds, and from worldly cares and concerns, that we might return to the comparative innocence of childhood. And yet it means so much more than this. We are called not only to turn away from all that is wrong with our "adult" approach to life, but also to turn towards all that is good and true in the life of a child; not only to put off our adult ways, but also to put on the ways of a child. Whenever and wherever possible, our approach to life is to be that of a little child. And this includes what we might think of as our "spiritual life".

We all desire to grow and mature in our faith, to enter more and more into the fullness of God's kingdom – and it's easy to believe that if only we could pray more or read our Bible more or meet more often for teaching and praise and

## *As a Child*

worship, then we might begin to draw closer to God and know more of his reality in our lives. But although we might protest otherwise, this is at heart a very adult approach to God and to our faith. We are endeavouring to achieve our goal by our own efforts; trying to get what we want by doing what we think we have to do.

This is not to say that such spiritual disciplines are unnecessary or unimportant; they are, of course, God's gifts to us, which have nourished and nurtured countless Christians throughout the ages. But they are not the key to the kingdom of heaven. This, Jesus tells us, is to be found in us becoming like little children, and in coming to him as little children. All that we do in order to grow and mature in our faith must be approached in the same way, with the attitude of a little child. If not, we risk missing out on the very thing that we seek, by leaving behind the childlike faith that opens the door to God's kingdom.

# Humbles

> Therefore, whoever **humbles** himself like this child is the greatest in the kingdom of heaven.[1]

Winston Churchill is reputed to have said of Clement Attlee, the post-war British Prime Minister, that he was "a modest man, who has much to be modest about." This was not, of course, intended to be taken as a compliment. Churchill was suggesting not that Attlee had many significant abilities and achievements about which he could be modest, but rather that his abilities and achievements were of such insignificance that modesty was the only appropriate response.

This typically amusing Churchillian put-down hints at what it means to be humble like a child – and this is something rather different from what we adults tend to think of as humility.

For adults, humility generally entails us playing down our abilities and achievements, and setting aside any advantages associated with our position and power. It is, if you like, behaving as if we did not have these things.

Let's be honest, humility such as this is not something that we see very often in little children. In part this is because they are too young to realise the necessity for humility, or even truly to understand what humility is. More to the point,

## As a Child

however, is the fact that there is little or nothing in their lives that they are able to play down or set aside, even if they wanted to; for their abilities are limited, their achievements are small, they have no position or power. To mimic Churchill's comment about Attlee, they are humble and they have much to be humble about.

As such, the humility of a little child is not so much an attitude of mind as a state of being, a fundamental part of whom and what they are. Indeed, the word "humble" can literally mean "not rising far from the ground", which is a perfect way to describe these "little ones", whose size dictates a very real physical humility: small, and powerless and weak.

In their letters, both Paul and Peter exhort the early believers to "clothe yourselves with humility."[2] This phrase is suggestive of what it means for adults to be humble: it is something that we "put on" – at best, from a desire not to "show off" what we are and what we have: at worst, simply to cover over our pride.

In contrast, childlike humility is not so much a "putting on" as a "putting off"; a giving up of our desire to have and our desire to be; a giving up, even, of what we have and what we are. To be truly humble like a child is to have few possessions, a lowly position, little power.

For this was the way taken by Jesus. His humility entailed an actual, physical change in his circumstances, a very real "coming down". His was the greatness and the power and the glory and the majesty and the splendour of God.[3] He had everything, yet he made himself nothing; he chose freely to give it all up, to let it all go. He set aside his divinity to take on our humanity. Leaving his eternal home with his Father in heaven, he came to live a life here on earth: a life of service and of obedience and ultimately of death on a cross.[4]

*Humbles*

And he came as a helpless baby, totally dependent upon his human parents for protection and provision, for all that he needed to survive and to grow. We are so familiar with this story that we seldom feel any shock at the idea of Almighty God making himself so vulnerable; we can hardly envisage things happening any other way. And yet Jesus could just as easily have appeared on earth as a fully grown man, ready to embark upon his adult ministry. Instead, he chose to share the full extent of our humanity and to show the endless depths of his humility, by becoming a little child.

Such an understanding of humility could have a profound effect on how we live out our faith. Many Christians and many churches desire to do something "significant" for God – and, of course, this is in many ways a laudable aim. But what this can translate to in practice is a desire to become significant ourselves: to gain more prominence and to increase our influence – not, of course, for our own sakes (perish the thought!), but rather that we might be better equipped to "impact" the world for God.

Now there is no doubt that there are individuals and churches that are called upon by God to take on such "significant" roles: to be high-profile, to be influential, to be "successful" – and far be it from me to call into question the reality of any such calling. I would, however, question whether this is the path that God wants most of us to take. In his letter to the church in Corinth, Paul tells us about the type of person that God chooses and uses to fulfil his purposes. And rarely is it those whom the world would consider to be wise or influential or important; rather, it's the foolish and the weak and the lowly and the despised. He chooses "the things that are not ... so that none may boast before him."[5]

## As a Child

What a telling phrase this is. We want to be "something", yet God chooses those who are "nothing". We fondly believe that the more we bring to God, the more he will be able to use us. But God doesn't need us to bring him anything; indeed, it seems he would almost prefer it if we didn't. For he is the One who delights in creating something out of nothing; who in the beginning spoke into the darkness and brought forth the heavens and the earth. How much more, then, is he able to produce whatever he desires from the "nothingness" of our lives. As others have said, the only ability that God requires of us is availability.

Speaking to his disciples of his impending death, Jesus said to them, "I tell you the truth, unless a kernel of wheat falls to the ground and dies, it remains only a single seed. But if it dies, it produces many seeds."[6] Fruitfulness and abundance, it seems, must come through humility and death: first and foremost through the death of Jesus, then through each of us dying to our own selfish ambitions and desires. Just as a seed is literally humbled in falling to the ground and entering the soil, so we in humbling ourselves come into that place from which true growth and increase will come. And throughout history there have been countless men and women of faith – the vast majority known only to God – who have done just this, and whose lives of humble service have been the channels through which God has touched and transformed the lives of individuals, families, communities, countries, even the whole world.

The kingdom of God is an upside-down kingdom, a topsy-turvy kingdom: where the first are last, and the last are first;[7] where the one who rules is like the one who serves;[8] where those who seem to be weaker are indispensable;[9] where those who exalt themselves will be humbled, and those who humble themselves will be exalted;[10] where the greatest is a little child.[11] If we truly desire to "make a difference for God" and see his kingdom come, then we need to do things God's way and not the world's way. There is no need for us to try and ape its attitudes or mimic its methods. Nor do we need to compete with the world in order to try to prove God's power, with an attitude of "Anything you can do, He can do better." Rather, we need to learn to walk the way of "insignificance", seeking to be "nothing" rather than desiring to be "something", learning to love and serve in gentleness and humility. If we are willing to do this then God himself will take care of any "significance" in what we do. After all, in the seeming insignificance and failure of his earthly life and death, Jesus achieved something of the greatest significance for all humanity, whose effect will be felt throughout all eternity.

# Enter

"I tell you the truth, unless you change and become like little children, you will never **enter** the kingdom of heaven."[1]

Whilst on holiday the other year we booked my daughter into a "high ropes adventure" activity. Not unreasonably there was an age restriction of eight years and over, but with my daughter soon to turn ten we did not anticipate that this would be a problem. Imagine her disappointment and our frustration when we arrived at the allotted time, only to discover that she also had to be at least 140cm tall (that's 4′ 8″ for those of us who still struggle with metric measurements) and just came up short.

It is perhaps little wonder that children are eager to grow up. They want to be taller, they want to be stronger, they want to be older. They long to be able to do all those things that at present they are unable to do. Teenagers, especially, are often impatient to enter into those places and practices that officially should be closed to them for a few years more – enjoying alcoholic drinks, going to night-clubs, watching adult-rated movies, driving a car; perhaps earning a full-time wage, or voting, or even getting married. The particulars may vary across countries and cultures, but such restrictions and reactions are common the whole world over.

## As a Child

In the Jewish tradition, for example, a boy is considered to be an adult when he turns 13 and becomes a Bar Mitzvah ("son of the Commandments"). Only then is he able fully to participate in the synagogue and other areas of Jewish community life. (For girls the age of adulthood is 12, although some more Orthodox traditions do not allow them to participate in synagogue meetings.) This is why it would have been so shocking to hear Jesus say that only the childlike could enter the kingdom of heaven; because if children were excluded from participating in the synagogue, how could they possibly be the pattern and model for those admitted to the kingdom itself?

Of course, it is not only age and physical size that determine eligibility for entry. University and college courses require specific qualifications from prospective students. Job advertisements ask for particular expertise and experience. Sporting contests demand standards of achievement from those seeking to compete. High-class hotels and exclusive holiday destinations are closed to those without wealth or connections. Even everyday leisure activities frequently require tickets or membership (and the money to pay for these). Most social events are by invitation only.

This tends to be how we think about entry requirements: they stipulate what it is you must have in order to get in. But not all entry requirements are like this. Sometimes it is not about what you have, but rather what you don't have.

When my children were younger we used to take them to indoor adventure play areas. I'm sure that many of you will know just what I mean: climbing frames and walkways and tunnels and slides and ball-pits and bouncy castles and more. There was nothing like this when I was a child, and I'd love to have a go now – but of course, I'm too old and too large and

*Enter*

too heavy (and probably too unfit). I'd not be able to squeeze myself through the confined spaces; the equipment could bend or break under my weight; I might inadvertently hurt a little child (or even myself!)

Play areas such as these are not designed to be used by adults (we are far too big) and so only children are permitted to enter. In the same way, entry into the kingdom of heaven is restricted to those who are willing to humble themselves, to make themselves small, and to become like little children. Only they are able to "squeeze their way" into the kingdom; only they will not damage what God has created; only they will not trample on those around them. For the kingdom is made for the childlike: this is the way God designed it to be. And the things that open doors in the world – power and strength, qualifications and achievements, expertise and experience, money and connections – will not gain us entry; indeed, they are more likely to be a hindrance, puffing us up and weighing us down.

Jesus said, "It is easier for a camel to go through the eye of a needle than for a rich man to enter the kingdom of God."[2] This is undoubtedly a somewhat surreal (some might say "Pythonesque") image, and there have been various attempts to explain it: that there was a gate known as the "Needle's Eye" in the walls of Jerusalem, so small that a camel would have to be unloaded and get down on its knees in order to get through; or that the Greek word *kamelos* meaning "camel" should really be *kamilos* meaning "cable" or "rope". Sadly, there is no evidence that such a gate ever existed, and the oldest and most reliable manuscripts do indeed use the word "camel".

In fact, all such explanations are unnecessary. The image that Jesus uses is meant to be improbable and implausible, is

## As a Child

meant to grab the listener's attention, and emphasise the extreme difficulty (some might say impossibility) of entering God's kingdom whilst encumbered by the world's riches. He deliberately juxtaposes the largest living creature known to his audience (the camel) with one of the smallest openings that they would encounter in daily life (the eye of a needle). Something so large can not possibly fit through something so small – and thus, in order to enter the kingdom you need to have less, you need to be less, you need to be small.

Jesus makes a similar point elsewhere, when he tells us to "enter through the narrow gate" (or "narrow door") and take the "narrow road."[3] In Matthew's account the emphasis seems to be on how difficult it is to find and travel "the road that leads to life" – and this tends to be the message that we take from this teaching. But in Luke's account the emphasis is slightly different: "Make every effort to enter through the narrow door, because many, I tell you, will try to enter and will not be able to." Here, the problem is not so much finding the "narrow door" as entering through it. Why should this be? The obvious answer, surely, is that those who try are just too big – too tall, or too wide – and they won't fit through the gap.

Entry into the kingdom is possible only for those who become like little children, for those who are prepared to make themselves small. All too often we want to be bigger, yet the reality is that we need to be smaller.

But little children do not show us only how we must enter the kingdom of God; they show us also how we might enter more fully into the life of the kingdom.

As a child I could play football for hours. I wasn't very good, but I enjoyed it – so much so that my brother and I would go out into our back garden, or across the road to the playing fields, and would not return inside until it was almost too dark to see. I would imagine myself to be the well-known players of the time (with no justification), and would re-enact the highlights that we'd just seen on television, with the stirring theme-tune resounding around my head. Sad to say, as a parent I'd go out into our garden for a kick-around with my children, and within half-an-hour or so I'd be beginning to flag. It's not simply that I'm too unfit and lacking in energy, more that I just don't get as caught-up and engrossed in the game as I once did.

As a family we've spent a few holidays on camp sites in northern France. One of our main criteria when choosing a site has been the provision of a good swimming pool area, complete with slides and flumes. The children will ride the slides again and again, finding countless ways to enjoy just being in the water – so much so that they apparently become immune to the cold, and seemingly would stay in the pool all day if allowed to do so. I too enjoy the pool, but I just don't have my children's staying power. I'll go down the slides a few times and have bit of a splash and a swim, but then I'm ready to get out and relax and read a book. In part this is because I'm beginning to chill off, but mainly it's because I've simply had enough, am beginning to get a little bored, and want to do something else.

As adults, rarely are we able to enter fully into what we are doing. There are always too many other things clamouring for our time and attention: things that we need to do, and things that we want to do. Familiarity dulls our interest. We get distracted. Our mind wanders. We move on.

God does not want us to be like this; rather, he wants us to enter into life in his kingdom like little children. We are to give ourselves to it wholeheartedly, immerse ourselves in it, be absorbed by it, give it all our energies, our full attention. We are to be to be so engaged with God and the things of God that nothing else matters. We are to "keep on keeping on" even when it's getting "cold and dark"; not simply out of duty and obedience (important as these are) but because we are so caught up in the kingdom that the difficulties and discomforts really are no discouragement. We keep on because we want to keep on. Not becoming bored and jaded by a daily repetition of old routines, but rather being re-envisioned and re-energised as we encounter more and more of the infinite variety of God's kingdom; as we appreciate more and more of how we are called and equipped to bring his kingdom into his world; and as we come to know more and more of the height and the depth and the length and the breadth of his love.[4]

# Believed

Yet to all who received him, to those who **believed** in his name, he gave the right to become children of God.[1]

In the book *Alice Through The Looking Glass* by Lewis Carroll there is a short exchange between Alice and the White Queen on the subject of belief. "I can't believe that!" says Alice, responding to the White Queen's claim that she is "one hundred and one, five months and a day," "one can't believe impossible things." "I daresay you haven't had much practice," says the Queen. "Why, sometimes I've believed as many as six impossible things before breakfast."

As Christians, many of us will have experienced periods of doubt during which it can feel as if holding on to our faith requires just such mental gymnastics. And if this is how it can sometimes seem for those who have seen at least something of the reality of God and his kingdom in our lives, just consider for a moment how hard belief must be for those who have not seen, and with whom we seek to share the good news of Jesus.

Indeed, I well remember when, in my late teens, I first began thinking about the meaning of "Life, the Universe and Everything" (as the writer Douglas Adams would have it), and discussing spiritual matters with a few school friends who

## As a Child

happened to go to church. My reaction at the time was just the same as Alice's: "one can't believe impossible things" – or, as I stated emphatically, "I can't make myself believe what I don't believe!"

Let's be honest, such a reaction is not altogether surprising: Jesus as both man and God, his birth to a virgin, his miracles and healings, his perfect and sinless life, his rising from the dead, indeed the very existence of God himself – there, that's "six impossible things" for starters! Then there's the explanation of why Jesus' life and death was necessary and what it all achieved: our rebellion against God, our fall from grace, the broken relationship, the need for justice, the perfect sacrifice, the price paid, death defeated, complete forgiveness, eternal life. It's a lot for someone to get their head around.

And yet I can't help but wonder if we don't have a tendency to over-complicate things. A few years ago a British bank ran an advertising campaign which focused on their claim that they provided simple and straightforward services, "because life's complicated enough". I can almost imagine Jesus making the same claim for the good news of his kingdom; this too is meant to be simple and straightforward – so simple and straightforward in fact that a little child can accept it. Indeed, not only can a little child accept it, but only a little child can accept it: for as Jesus says, "anyone who will not receive the kingdom of God like a little child will never enter it."[2]

But let's be honest, most young children would seem to have little or no concept of what the good news of the kingdom is really all about; and this being the case, how can they possibly accept something they don't understand? The obvious answer is that they don't really accept it at all, they

*Believed*

just blindly believe whatever they are told – and that therefore their belief in God is really no different from their belief in, say, Father Christmas or the Tooth Fairy.

Whilst there is undoubtedly some truth in this, it would be wrong to conclude that this somehow invalidates a little child's acceptance of God and his kingdom. The authenticity of their childlike faith rests upon the reality of God, not upon the depth of their understanding.

We all too readily reduce the good news to a set of statements to be believed, a series of assertions to be accepted; but this is not what it is meant to be at all. Indeed, much of the message that we feel we have to communicate is not, in fact, an integral part of the good news of Jesus. Rather, it comes in large part from the New Testament letters and, as such, was written not to explain the faith to non-believers, but to help the members of the early Church understand what they had already accepted. It was written, in other words, to encourage those who already had a faith in Jesus, not to convince those who did not.

None of which is to suggest that what we believe about the good news is unimportant, or that you have to abandon your intellect and understanding and leave your brain behind when you become a Christian. But intellectual knowledge is not the key to the kingdom; indeed, I suspect that very few people are actually convinced into a belief that the good news is true.

Some years back I was involved in leading the Alpha course that our church put on for people wanting to explore the Christian faith. As we prepared for one course, the phrase "taste and see that the LORD is good" came to mind.[3] Our sense was very much that people would come to faith not so much through what was said in the talks, or through having

## As a Child

their questions answered during the discussions afterwards, but through seeing and experiencing the reality of God in their own lives and in the lives of others involved with the course.

I committed my life to God whilst still not truly believing any of the "impossible things" that had seemed such a stumbling block to me coming to faith. As I had argued with my friends, I had indeed been unable to make myself believe what I didn't believe. But I had got to the point (or rather, as I see now, God had brought me to the point) where I was able to accept that it might just possibly be true – and, if so, I ought to do something about it. And so, still unbelieving, I prayed to this God who might not exist, and offered my life to him if he did. At the time I felt no different. But the next day, speaking of what I had done, I was suddenly filled with an assurance that it was indeed true. For me, this was my personal experience of Paul's promise to the church in Corinth: "Now it is God who makes both us and you stand firm in Christ. He anointed us, set his seal of ownership on us, and put his Spirit in our hearts as a deposit, guaranteeing what is to come."[4]

It would be wrong, of course, to build a theology on one's own personal experiences; nonetheless, I do think this illustrates an important point. We tend to feel that people will not come to faith unless they truly believe the good news of Jesus, having arrived at a conviction and a confidence that it is true. But a belief such as this is not, primarily, the result of human reasoning: it is the work of God's Holy Spirit in a person's life. Rather than being a precondition of commitment, frequently it comes only after a person has chosen to give their life to God.

For we are called not to believe a doctrine, but to believe

*Believed*

in Jesus. It is a belief, not in something, but in someone. It is like a people believing in their President, or an army believing in its commander. Perhaps more pertinently, it is like a child believing in her parents, believing that they are in control, that they know what is best and will look after her. It is not so much a head-knowledge as a heart-response. It is saying to Jesus, "I will put my trust in you, and seek to follow where you lead."

# Revealed

"I praise you, Father, Lord of heaven and earth, because you have hidden these things from the wise and learned, and **revealed** them to little children."[1]

One of the more significant moments of my journey of faith came not in a church, nor at a conference, nor indeed in any religious context – but rather, in a car, returning from a weekend cycling with friends in the Black Mountains of South Wales.

At the time I was not in the best of places so far as my faith was concerned. After twenty or so years as a Christian I seemed to be no closer to God and no closer to becoming the person that I felt I was meant to be. This was not simply frustrating and disappointing; it also raised questions about the reality of the God whom I sought to follow. For if, after all this time, God seemed no more real to me, and had apparently produced few real changes in my character, this did rather call into question whether God was really there at all. In truth, the situation was not quite as stark as this description might suggest; I don't think that I was close to losing my faith, but it was all rather unsettling.

My journey home from this cycling weekend was with someone whom, at the time, I didn't know particularly well, and a four hour drive afforded us ample opportunity to learn a little more about each other. We spoke of our backgrounds, our jobs, our families, our faith – and as we chatted I found myself likening my faltering journey of faith to my journey down to Wales a couple of days previously.

Despite our hope that we might miss the worst of Friday's rush-hour there had been the usual congestion on the M25 London orbital motorway, and it took us almost two hours to travel the 60 or so miles round to the junction with the M4 motorway. We joined the M4 and drove west across England for another couple of hours, crossing the Severn Bridge and into south Wales. Soon we left the motorway and took the main road north, heading towards the eastern fringes of the Brecon Beacons National Park. Within half-an-hour or so we found ourselves driving down narrow, winding lanes, with hills and mountains rising around us. We were now nearing our destination, and before long we turned into a driveway that led up to our accommodation for the weekend: an old stone barn within sight of the ruins of Llanthony Priory, the arches of which framed magnificent views of the Black Mountains beyond.

I had never stayed here before, and on setting out on our journey earlier that day I'd had very little idea of what I was going to find there. After two hours spent crawling around the M25 I'd been none the wiser; and a further two hours later, though now in Wales, I'd still had no clearer view of where we were headed. On the final leg of our journey, driving up into the Brecon Beacons, the changing scenery had offered hints of what I might find, but it was only as we reached the top of the driveway, and finally arrived at our destination, that I truly saw what it was like.

And the thing that I realised as I journeyed home – the thing that utterly transformed the way that I felt about my

*Revealed*

faith — was simply this: you can travel an entire journey without your destination becoming clearer to you than it was when you set out, and it matters not a jot; your destination will be there just the same, and your journey will get you there just the same.

In the same way, I realised, the authenticity of my journey of faith did not depend upon the clarity of my vision of God, but upon the reality of God himself. I might spend the whole of my life knowing no more of God than I did then (or than I do now) and ultimately it would not matter; God will be who he is just the same, and one day I will see him just the same.

In many ways the frustration we might feel at an apparent lack of progress on our journey of faith is not unlike the impatience of a little child on a long car journey, crying out "Are we there yet?" Like them, we do not know the route we are taking, or the significance of the landmarks along the way, for it is a road we have never travelled before. And like them, all we can do is trust that our heavenly Father is taking us forward, is guiding us in the right direction, and that we will arrive at our destination all in good time.

As the apostle Peter wrote in his first letter, "Though you have not seen him, you love him; and even though you do not see him now, you believe in him and are filled with an inexpressible and glorious joy, for you are receiving the goal of your faith, the salvation of your souls."[2] Though we have not seen him, and do not see him, yet we believe, and still we receive.

This realisation, that I did not need to "see" Jesus and feel that I was drawing closer to him, quickly lead on to another, equally significant revelation. Just as I had expected to grow closer to God as I grew in my Christian faith, so too had I expected to grow in my knowledge and understanding of him. But now I began to appreciate that my knowledge and understanding were so limited and so partial that they were as nothing when set alongside the absolute truth of the full and unbounded reality of God. Furthermore, I realised, even the little knowledge and understanding that I thought I had was by no means certain and secure, since how could I be sure that it might not one day be eclipsed by some new revelation? All of which led me to a strong sense that I really knew nothing of God – a phrase that I would use repeatedly over the coming weeks and months.

Now you might reasonably assume that such thoughts would only add to my feelings of doubt and discouragement – but far from it. Perhaps somewhat surprisingly, they actually brought me great freedom and joy. It is very easy to slip into the error of building one's faith on the shifting sands of our own experience and understanding, rather than on the immovable rock of God. The realisation (or revelation) that I did not know – and could not know – was liberating. It redirected the focus from how I felt I was doing in my "walk of faith", and back on to the great "I AM", the One who is who he is, regardless of whom I might understand him to be. It released "my" God from the box of my understanding, and released me from the need to understand.

This is not to suggest, of course, that knowledge and understanding are wrong in themselves. As I have said previously, God doesn't want us to leave our brains behind when we become Christians. Indeed, our faith should act as a springboard to encourage and enable us to grapple with the difficult questions of life. The problem comes when we begin to use our knowledge to define boundaries and proscribe

*Revealed*

limits and reduce possibilities; to believe that the way we perceive something is the way that it actually is.

To be fair, it is perhaps understandable that we feel the need do this with what – we come to realise – is a complex, changeable and capricious world. We want to feel that we have some semblance of control, and so in our minds we reduce the world to a more manageable size – in effect, putting the world in a box. But in the same way (and perhaps for the same reason) we often use our knowledge of God to do the same with him, reducing God to a more manageable size and putting him in a box.

Little children do not go in for such box building. Yes, they have a voracious appetite for knowledge, but they do not share the adult compulsion to contain and control, to set boundaries and limits. They know that there is so much more to know, always new lands to discover beyond the horizon. They do not put the world in a box – and neither do they put God in a box.

Many of us will have heard it said, "Your God is too small."[3] Our instinctive response to this challenge tends to be to think that we need to extend our spiritual horizons – to attempt, in effect, to build a bigger box. But we don't need a bigger box – we need no box, for no box is big enough to contain the One who is "the Alpha and the Omega, the First and the Last, the Beginning and the End."[4] We can not grasp God. We can not truly know the unknowable. Our minds can not contain the uncontainable. As Solomon prayed when dedicating the temple in Jerusalem, "The heavens, even the highest heaven, cannot contain you. How much less this temple I have built!"[5] And how much less any box that we build from our own understanding.

The apostle Paul tells us that the letter kills, but the Spirit

## As a Child

gives life.[6] He is, of course, contrasting the old and new covenants, but he might equally be contrasting the rigidity of thought often exhibited by adults with the freedom of thought exhibited by children. Without realising it, we can drift into a "painting by numbers" view of the world – and of God – where we aim to colour in the missing pieces in our knowledge and understanding in the hope of completing the picture. The result is something that might bear a passing resemblance to reality, but which lacks all subtlety and vitality. Contrast this with the drawings and paintings of little children. These might be "wrong" in the technical sense – people with arms growing out of their heads seems to be a favoured "mistake" for some reason – and yet they are full of truth and life.

Jesus praises his Father for "[hiding] these things from the wise and learned, and [revealing] them to little children." The things hidden and revealed are not knowledge or understanding in the intellectual sense, but rather those deeper truths that call forth a heartfelt response. We supposedly wise and learned adults seek knowledge and understanding, thinking that this will bring us closer to God; but we would do well to heed Jesus' warning: "You diligently study the Scriptures because you think that by them you possess eternal life. These are the Scriptures that testify about me, yet you refuse to come to me to have life."[7] Learning can point us to Jesus, but does not, in itself, bring us any closer to him. The little children might lack knowledge, but God reveals to them what it important, and they come to Jesus and follow him simply because they are attracted by who he is and what he does.

The kingdom of heaven cannot be taken hold of by force of intellect; indeed, it is hidden by God from those who

*Revealed*

think themselves wise and leaned. Rather, it must be revealed by God himself, to those who come to him with the openness of little children.

# Receive

I tell you the truth, anyone who will not **receive** the kingdom of God like a little child will never enter it."[1]

As we have seen, acceptance of God and his kingdom is not so much concerned with intellectual assent, as with an instinctive and intuitive response to Jesus: it is less about the mind, and much more about the heart. For Jesus does not say here that we are to believe the kingdom; rather he says that we are to receive the kingdom. We are called not to believe a doctrine but to receive the free gift that God offers us in Jesus.[2] And we are to do so like little children, receiving God's kingdom just as a little child would receive any other gift: eagerly, excitedly, thankfully, joyfully. No concern about the motivation, no embarrassment about the generosity, no worries about what to give in return; just a simple, open-handed, open-hearted acceptance of the gift that is given.

But the need to receive the kingdom as a little child does not end with conversion and commitment. God's purpose is not that we receive a "golden ticket" that grants us entry to the kingdom when Jesus comes again. The kingdom is not simply something that is to come but something that has come and continues to come, breaking into the world here and now. Yes, we receive the kingdom when we choose to

*As a Child*

follow Jesus, but we are to continue to receive the kingdom, day-by-day, moment-by-moment – receiving the opportunities that unfold before us, and the resources that God supplies, in order that we might live out the new life that he has given us.

I write this chapter with Christmas fast approaching. Children, of course, love Christmas. They count down the days, many marking their passing by opening the doors on an Advent calendar (and, increasingly, eating the chocolate they find within). There are just so many things for children to enjoy and get excited about: the tree, the decorations, the lights; Father Christmas and his reindeer; the exchange of cards with their friends; perhaps a nativity play at school and a pantomime at the theatre. But of course, top of the list for most is the anticipation of the gifts they'll be given on Christmas morning. Many, indeed, will have started making a present-list weeks, if not months before, itemising all the things that they hope to receive.

Young children rarely have any trouble filling their Christmas list with all manner of gift ideas (many of which their parents might consider of dubious quality and value). But as they get older, they tend to ask for fewer (if more expensive) items. As an adult in my 40s I am now at a point where I ask for very little, for there really is very little that I want – and when it comes to material possessions, this is probably no bad thing. But I do wonder if this lack of desire has, perhaps, spilled over into the rest of my life – and, in particular, into my life of faith. I fear that I may have become too easily satisfied with what I have already received from God, and may have lost my heart-felt desire to receive more of him and his kingdom.

*Receive*

The Bible is full of warnings against the "many foolish and harmful desires that plunge men into ruin and destruction."[3] But desire in itself is not wrong; it is misplaced desire that is wrong. Perhaps some of us need to learn to desire again, to allow ourselves to desire again; to have that childlike longing to receive – not to receive the things of the world, but to receive the things of God.

The Psalms are full of such heart-felt desire: "As the deer pants for streams of water, so my soul pants for you, O God,"[4] "My soul thirsts for you, my body longs for you."[5] The prophet Isaiah declares, "Your name and renown are the desire of our hearts."[6] The apostle Paul counselled the Corinthian church to "eagerly desire spiritual gifts."[7]

Children expect to receive gifts from their parents at Christmas and on their birthdays. Such an attitude can, of course, lead to selfishness and ingratitude; but it can also be indicative of the depth of relationship between parent and child, that they know their parents want to give them good gifts. And in the same way, surely it is better to expect too much of God than to expect too little? For as Jesus said, "If you, then, though you are evil, know how to give good gifts to your children, how much more will your Father in heaven give good gifts to those who ask him!"[8]

But it is one thing to desire gifts; it's quite another to be ready to receive them. My young daughter does not have a large bedroom; in fact, she has to make do with the boxroom, one of the smallest rooms in the house. There is space for a bed, a wardrobe, a storage unit, and not much more. (She is looking forward to her eldest brother leaving home, in anticipation of being able to requisition his room!) This is somewhat unfortunate, as she quite possibly has more "stuff" than either her parents or her brothers, with the consequence that her things have to be stored throughout the rest of the house. Even so, her bedroom is still requires repeated clear-outs in order to keep it vaguely neat and tidy, and to ensure that there is some space available for all the new things that she receives.

For, of course, we can not truly receive something if we have nowhere to put it; if our rooms – or our lives – are too full of other things. And whilst little children may need some parental encouragement to make room to receive physical possessions, we have much to learn from them when it comes to being ready to receive things that are of far greater value and importance.

Jesus promised his followers life in all its fullness.[9] Yet we tend to be so full of ourselves and our thoughts and our desires that we have little room to receive the life that God has for us. Most little children are not like this. They are not preoccupied with themselves and caught up in themselves, not full of their own self-image and self-importance, not full of preconceptions and prejudices. They are not full of themselves and so they have room to receive: room to receive new experiences, room to receive new knowledge, room to receive new relationships, room to receive love and affection, room to receive all that life has to offer them.

We can know God's fullness only if we have this childlike capacity to receive. To be so empty of self that we have room to receive all the blessings that God has in store for us: room to receive God as our Father, room to receive Jesus as our saviour, room to receive the Holy Spirit as our guide and our counsellor, room to receive all the fullness of God and his kingdom.

*Receive*

And then, having received, we need to be willing to let go. We need to let go in order to pass on to others the blessings that we have ourselves received; and we need to let go in order that might have room to receive the new blessings that God has in store for us.

Here again, we have much to learn from little children. Of course there are times when they manage to take hold of something that they want, and no amount of cajoling or coercion seems likely to remove it from them. In such circumstances perhaps the best way to prise whatever it is from the unwilling child is to give them something else. For little children are much less concerned than most adults about holding on to what they have, and much more interested in receiving whatever new thing is offered to them.

We adults hold what we have tightly, for fear that it might be taken from us; little children hold what they have lightly, ready to receive the new and greater gifts to come, the blessings that each new moment brings. And in their receiving, little children enable us to receive also. Just consider the pleasure that we find in watching a little child experience all that life has to offer, finding such excitement and joy and pleasure in the seemingly smallest of things: sights and sounds and smells and textures and tastes. As they receive, so we receive through them.

William Blake encapsulates perfectly these two different ways of receiving — the adult and the child — in his short poem "Eternity":

He who bends to himself a joy
Does the wingèd life destroy;
But he who kisses the joy as it flies
Lives in eternity's sunrise.

# Belongs

"Let the little children come to me, and do not hinder them, for the kingdom of heaven **belongs** to such as these."[1]

When I was younger my dad had a rather nice record deck. Not unreasonably he wasn't keen on the idea of me and my brothers using and abusing it, so it was strictly "off limits" – at least until we were older and had learnt how to treat it properly. If we wanted to play our records, then we had our own (rather cheaper) record player; or we could ask Dad if he would mind putting our records on his deck.

Some people regard the kingdom of heaven in much the same way. They think that the things of the kingdom are reserved for those who are older, wiser and more mature in their faith. Some even believe that the only way they can have access to God and his kingdom is through the ministries of priests or elders or other church leaders – rather in the same way that we children could use Dad's record deck only by asking him to put the records on for us. Even if this is not what we truly believe, we can still find ourselves thinking and behaving as if this were the case – hanging on to the coat-tails of "famous" and "successful" teachers and healers and worship-leaders, as if it were only through their ministries and ministrations that we truly expect to hear and receive and

## As a Child

encounter the living God.

But this is not what Jesus says. Rather, all of the riches and resources of the kingdom are freely available – without restriction or reservation – to all who come to God as little children; for the kingdom, we are told, "belongs to such as these."

But why should this be? Why should the kingdom belong to the childlike in particular?

First and foremost, these are the ones who feel most deeply that their true home is to be found in the kingdom of heaven. Of course, all believers are members of God's household,[2] and find their home with him. Yet some of us behave more like adolescent teenagers, pushing boundaries and craving independence; or else like young adults, outwardly conforming to the "house rules" yet inwardly hankering after a place of our own, where we are free to live how we choose. Little children are not like this. They know that their home is with their parents: this is where they belong, this is where they will find love and care and protection. And, in the same way, the childlike know that they belong in the kingdom, at home with their heavenly Father, and they have no desire to be anywhere else.

The kingdom of heaven belongs to the childlike just as our family home belongs to my children. It is not that they are the legal owners – indeed, I doubt very much they would welcome having to pay the mortgage! Rather, it belongs to them because, as our children and as a part of our family, they have the right to live here. Indeed, so much more than the right, which suggests some sense of grudging obligation; rather, as their mum and dad we delight to have them with us. They belong in the family home and, as such, the family home belongs to them.

*Belongs*

In the same way, Jesus assures us, as God's children we belong in his Father's house – so much so that he himself has gone to prepare a place for us, that we might be with him where he is.[3] Imagine that! Jesus, the King of kings and Lord of lords getting your room ready for you. And this place in his kingdom belongs to us by right – not because of anything that we have done to earn it or deserve it, but simply as adopted sons and daughters of God. As the apostle Paul wrote to the churches in Galatia, "God sent his Son ... that we might receive the full rights of sons."[4]

Of course, we will fully inherit our heavenly home only when, at the last, we go to be with Jesus; and yet, it belongs to us here and now. The kingdom of heaven is our true home, the family home, our home as children of our heavenly Father. It is where we abide and where we rest, where we are fed and where we grow, where we know love and where we feel secure, the place from which we go out into the world and the place to which we return.

It is the Church, the fellowship of believers, the body of Christ. But it is so much more than this. It is wherever God finds a welcome in the world and wherever he finds a welcome in our lives. As we make our home with God in his kingdom, so he makes his home with us[5] and forms his kingdom within us.[6] This is the measure of what he has given; this is how much the kingdom belongs to us: it becomes a very part of us. We belong in God's kingdom and his kingdom belongs in us.

But not only does God give the childlike a home in his kingdom, he gives them all of its riches and resources also. As Paul wrote to the church in Rome, "[God] did not spare his own Son, but gave him up for us all – how will he not also, along with him, graciously give us all things?"[7] There are no age restrictions, nothing is out of bounds – the childlike can have it all.

But can this really be the case? Would God really give the things of the kingdom to those who will treat them like little children? After all, as parents it would be irresponsible of us to allow our children to play with anything and everything within our home. There are things that we must keep from them, both for their own protection and to keep our possessions safe from harm.

Because let's be realistic about this: little children tend not to be very good at looking after the things they are given. They bash them and drop them and throw them around, and try to use them in ways for which they were never designed. Their toys get broken, their books get bent, their clothes get torn. They have little or no idea of the value of what they have, and rarely look after their possessions as they should. Does Jesus really mean that the kingdom of God belongs to such as these? Surely they can't be trusted and entrusted with something of such worth?

Now without doubt, as the perfect parent, God does at times withhold things from us until we are truly ready to receive them and use them properly. Yet many a time he is far more willing to give to those who have a childlike approach than to those who are more grown up in their handling of what they've been given.

Like many young boys, as a child I had quite a collection of die-cast model vehicles. I raced them across the room, crashed them into walls and each other, even flew them through the air; then I scooped them up and dropped them together in a drawer, or left them scattered across the floor, waiting to be crushed beneath some-one's feet. Inevitably,

## Belongs

after a while they became rather the worse for wear: the paintwork got chipped, the windows got scratched, the wheels got bent.

Today these same toys are marketed and sold as "collectibles", and early models in pristine condition can be worth a small fortune – especially if they are still in their original packaging. "If only I'd been more careful!" I might think. Adult collectors would never dream of treating these models with the same casual disregard that I did as a child. They are properly looked after and protected from damage. Displayed in cabinets like ornaments or even shut up in boxes and stored safely away, there's no chance of them ending up in the same state as my childhood toys. And yet it seems wrong, somehow, for any toy to be treated like this: never having been played with by a child, never having fired his imagination, never having elicited her affection, never having brought a youngster pleasure and joy, never having fulfilled the purpose for which it was created.

Jesus tells a famous story of a man who went on a journey, entrusting money to his three servants.[8] Two of the servants used what they'd been given to make more money for their master, and were commended for their efforts. The third, however, hid the money in the ground, returning it with the words, "I was afraid ... See here is what belongs to you." Hearing the tale for the first time we might reasonably expect that this servant would receive at least some credit for keeping his master's money safe and returning it intact. But not a bit of it. Instead, he receives nothing but condemnation. Why? Because he has made no use of what he's been given.

It is all too easy for us to fall into behaving like this third servant, so fearful of failure and loss that we fail to use the gifts that we've been given. We are only too well aware of the

## As a Child

value of what we have, and of how fragile and fleeting it can be. This applies not only to our physical possessions, but perhaps more especially to those far more precious things: our family and friends, our health and happiness, our time and activities, our hopes and dreams – all that life entails, and ultimately life itself.

And so we play it safe. We look to protect what we have. Preservation becomes our first priority. Rather than using all we've been given, we bury it in the ground.

We might not admit it – perhaps even to ourselves – but as Christians we can be especially fearful of losing the very thing that makes us what we are – our faith in Christ. We fear that we may be tested and found wanting, that we may be seduced by the undoubted attractions of the world, that our faith may crumble and fall if we allow our foundation of simple certainties to be undermined. And so we shy away from encountering the world as it really is – with all its complexities and contradictions, its certainties and doubts, its sorrows and joys. We shut ourselves up in a box – in our godly ghetto, our holy huddle – to keep ourselves safe and secure. Just witness the siege mentality that the church so often adopts when it feels threatened by the world.

But, paradoxically, in seeking to protect and preserve our life and faith in this way, we can end up losing the very thing that we are trying to keep. Like the servant in the parable, if we do not use what has been entrusted to us, it will be taken from us. As Jesus warns us, "Whoever wants to save his life will lose it, but whoever loses his life for me will save it."[9]

And so, we need to be like little children: not keeping the myriad gifts that we've been given shut up "safely" in their boxes, but delighting to use them all with childlike abandon – for "the kingdom of heaven belongs to such as these."

# Called

Jesus **called** the children to him…[1]

Jesus was forever calling out to people. He called children to come to him. He called crowds to listen and understand his message.[2] He called the sick to be healed,[3] and the dead to be raised to life.[4] He called four fishermen to follow him, promising to make them "fishers of men".[5] He called twelve apostles, giving them power and authority to drive out demons and to cure diseases, and sending them out to preach the kingdom of God and to heal the sick.[6] He called all kinds of people in order that he might transform their lives and so empower them to transform the lives of others.

Perhaps in part because of this we tend to attach a great deal of importance to the whole concept of "calling". We are encouraged to "consider our calling" and to "discover God's plan" for our lives. Countless books have been written on the subject and countless sermons preached. There are courses and conferences, studies and seminars. There are even personality tests that promise to provide an insight into our character and gifting, and hence some indication of our calling. We talk about it and we pray about it. We ask ourselves, "Just what does God have in store for me? What does he want me to do?"

This concern with our calling arises from the very best of intentions: from a desire to identify the ways in which God might wish to use us, and in which we might best use our gifts and abilities to further his kingdom; to help us to see that we each have a unique part to play; to encourage and challenge us to step out in faith and make a difference in the world.

Unfortunately the effect of such introspection can be the very opposite of what is intended. Far from helping and encouraging us, it can instead leave us feeling frustrated and disappointed: frustrated that we don't seem able to hear God's call on our lives, and disappointed as we conclude that perhaps this means he has no particular use for us.

It might be all very well for those who have a strong sense of calling, such as those whose job is also their vocation (a word rooted in the Latin for "voice", and so literally meaning "what the voice called you to do"). But many others – myself included – feel no such call. We are where we are and do what we do, not because we have responded to some specific calling, but simply because … well, just because.

For example, at present I work in the City of London for a Lloyd's underwriting agents (yes, you might well ask!) My position there is not, I can assure you, something that I ever aimed to achieve or planned to do. It just happens to be where I've ended up, something that I've found my way into. It is a role that makes use of my abilities, experience and knowledge. I find it challenging and satisfying (although not, of course, all of the time). And, for me most importantly of all, it provides the income to support my family. It is, in a word, my job. I trust that God is with me in it and uses me through it, but in no way would I consider it to be a calling

*Called*

or vocation.

Indeed, to be quite truthful, I really don't have specific goals in life that I strive to achieve. My approach has always been more to take opportunities as they arise rather than to make opportunities happen. My epitaph might read, "Let's just see how things pan out"! I'm not sure that this is necessarily any better or worse than a more directed approach; it is just different. Some sense a clear calling and vision and some don't – that's just how it is.

But such a specific sense of calling is just one facet of the far greater and wider-ranging call that God makes to us and upon our lives. And we can see this perhaps most clearly in Jesus' calling of children.

For when Jesus called the children, he did so not in order to give them some specific task or role. He did not call them do anything or to be anything, but simply to be with him. "Let the little children come to me."[7] And the children came, not because they hoped to hear his plan for their lives or be envisioned and empowered to fulfil his purposes, but simply because they were attracted by his life and by his love, and they wanted to be around him.

This too is our primary calling: to come to Jesus and to be with him – not in some complex, mystical, spiritual sense, and not for any particular purpose, but simply as a little child would come to her father or mother or sister or brother; for no other reason that this is family, this is where she belongs, and she wants to be with them.

In his account of the early Church, Luke records that "when they [the rulers and elders and teachers of the law] saw the courage of Peter and John and realised that they were unschooled, ordinary men, they were astonished and they took note that these men had been with Jesus."[8] For all that

*As a Child*

the apostles went on to achieve for the kingdom of God, it began with this simple yet fundamental fact: they had been with Jesus. This is the call that comes before all others, upon which all other calls are founded, and from which all other callings flow.

Secondly, Jesus called the children simply to be themselves: "He called a little child and had him stand among them."⁹ Jesus called this little child to proclaim the truth and reality of the kingdom of God, not only to the crowd gathered on that day, but to all who would hear and read and receive this gospel account throughout all the years that would follow. Quite a calling. Yet the little child did not have to say or do anything special; indeed, he did not have to say or do anything at all. He simply had to stand among crowd and be himself, be the person that God had created, be a little child.

In the same way, before God calls us to do anything particular, he calls us simply to stand as a witness to the people amongst whom we find ourselves; to stand as the person that he has created us to be, as the person that he is recreating in Christ, as a person who is receiving and revealing the kingdom of God as a little child.

None of which is to suggest that God does not call individuals (and groups) to fulfil particular tasks or take on particular roles – of course he does. The Bible is full of such stories, as is the history of the Church down through the ages, and God continues to call his people to serve him in specific ways, both "great" and "small". Neither is it to say that God might not call you or I in such a way, nor that we need not be attentive and responsive to any such call – of course he might and of course we must. Indeed, even I, for all my lack of vision, have had times where I have felt, "This is

*Called*

where God wants me to be right now, this is what he wants me to do."

Yet if we become preoccupied with the task of trying to "discover our calling" then we run the risk of missing all that God has already called us to be. He has called us to belong to Jesus,[10] to be in fellowship with him,[11] and to be transformed into his likeness.[12] He has called us to be holy,[13] to endure suffering,[14] to be a blessing to others,[15] and to be a people of peace.[16] He has called us to freedom,[17] and to hope,[18] and to life eternal.[19] He has called us heavenward,[20] out of darkness into light,[21] that we might share in Christ's glory.[22]

What a calling this is! If we could but truly hear it and receive it and respond to it, what a difference it would make, both to ourselves and to all who would then see the reality of God's kingdom revealed in us. This is our ultimate calling: to come to Jesus as little children, to receive his kingdom as little children and to live our lives as true children of our heavenly Father.

# Obedient

As **obedient** children, do not conform to the evil desires you had when you lived in ignorance.[1]

When my daughter turned 11 she received a birthday card that proclaimed, "'Getting older is fun, it means you don't have to do what you're told.' (Molly, aged 6)". This young child's remark makes us smile because, even as grown-ups, we recognise the truth of it. For children are forever being told what to do, forever having their lives ordered by others. From when to get up to when to go to bed, and all points in between: eat this food, wear these clothes, go to school, do this work, come here, go there, do this, don't do that, and so on and so on. Of course, as adults our days are far from wholly our own but, nonetheless, most of us would struggle to cope with even a fraction of the commands and demands that children are expected to follow, with their lack of autonomy and self-determination.

Perhaps this is why some of us struggle with the whole concept — still less the practice — of obedience to God. Instinctively we agree with Molly: we're grown-ups now and old enough decide for ourselves how we live our lives. We don't need or want anyone else — even God — telling us what to do.

## As a Child

Little children need to be told what to do because they do not yet have the experience and maturity to make wise and appropriate decisions for themselves. They need looking after and they need a strong guiding hand. And in some ways this is true of us as children of God. Our heavenly Father knows far better than we do how we should live our lives, and he wants to protect us from situations and behaviour that would be damaging to ourselves or to others. It is in our very best interests to open our ears to his instructions and commands – through his word, through the words of others, through the prompting of his Holy Spirit, though whatever means he chooses – and to respond with the obedience of little children.

But in seeking obedience from our children, those of us who are parents are doing more than trying to ensure that they do the right thing here and now, in this or that situation. More importantly, we are trying to prepare them for the future, to teach them how to behave, to know "right from wrong," to be able to make those wise and appropriate decisions for themselves. As the book of Proverbs counsels, "Train a child in the way he should go, and when he is old he will not turn from it."[2] We seek to train our children in obedience in the hope that they will choose to walk in obedience.

For true obedience is to be found, not so much in doing as we are told, as in doing for ourselves what we already know to be right. As Paul wrote to the church in Ephesus, "Slaves, obey your earthly masters ... not only to win their favour when their eye is on you, but like slaves of Christ, doing the will of God from your heart."[3] If this is how it was to be between slaves and their masters, how much more should it be between children and their parents, and between children of God and their heavenly Father.

As parents, we don't want forever to be telling our children what to do and when to do it, to be making all their decisions for them. Rather, we want them more and more to take responsibility for themselves, to make their own way in the world, to flourish and to grow as the individuals that God has created them to be. Yes, we will always be there for them, ready to offer our advice and counsel if it is needed and asked for, but we will no longer be directing and determining their lives as we once did. And this is how it should be.

In the same way, I believe, God does not want us to become mindlessly dependent on him, forever asking him what to do, never making any decisions ourselves, never taking any responsibility ourselves. Rather, as our perfect parent, he wants us to grow in our faith, to be "trained in obedience," so that increasingly we will know and choose for ourselves "the way we should go." As Paul wrote to the church in Rome, "Be transformed by the renewing of your mind. Then your will be able to test and approve what God's will is – his good, pleasing and perfect will."[4]

In the book of Deuteronomy we find the following promise and encouragement from God to his people, "Now what I am commanding you today is not too difficult for you or beyond your reach ... No, the word is very near you; it is in your mouth and in your heart so that you may obey it."[5] God has told us how to live through his commandments. He has placed this word in our heart by his Holy Spirit. Now we are not to sit wondering and worrying about what to do, but rather to set off to walk in obedience, trusting that he will be there at our shoulder to help us stay on the straight and narrow. "Whether you turn to the right or to the left, your ears will hear a voice behind you, saying, This is the way;

## As a Child

walk in it."[6]

Jesus said that he had come that we might have life in all its fullness;[7] yet, as a friend so astutely observed, too often Christianity looks more like life in all its emptiness. Like children over-anxious to please their parents we can be paralysed into inaction; so desperate to do right (or not do wrong) that we do nothing. But God, I believe, is far more frustrated by our inaction than he is by the mistakes that we make in trying to live our lives.

Jesus came and lived and died to enable us to live and make mistakes. Not that we should deliberately sin, or put ourselves into the path of temptation ("By no means!" says Paul.[8]) But were there no forgiveness in and through Jesus, we would indeed be paralysed by the fear of doing wrong – although our inaction would, of course, be sin itself ("in the evil we have done and the good we have not done"[9]). But because of Jesus we can go out into the world and live, seeking to bring his life and light into the deadness and darkness, risking failure and mistakes, because we know that he will not condemn us, but rather forgive us, restore us and set us right.

But of course, there are times when God wants us to obey not just his universal commands to all people, but also his specific direction for us as individuals – and I know that I for one have a long way to go when it comes to learning to listen and being willing to obey. I must admit to having a certain fondness for Jonah who, when God told him, "Go to the great city of Nineveh and preach against it," instead "ran away from the LORD and headed for Tarshish."[10] I strongly suspect that I would have done the same.

But the more we learn to be obedient to God's universal

## Obedient

commands, the more we will be prepared to obey when he gives us specific direction. And this may even have been true of Jesus: for the writer of the book of Hebrews tells us, "Although he was a son, he learned obedience from what he suffered."[11]

At first sight this would seem to suggest that before Jesus "learned obedience" he must have been disobedient. But this can not be right because the same writer tells us that Jesus was "tempted in every way, just as we are – yet was without sin."[12] So it is not that Jesus was ever disobedient, but rather that his obedience reached new levels in his suffering and death on the cross. The self-denial and self-sacrifice that was asked of him by his heavenly Father was more than had ever been asked of him before; was more indeed, that had ever, or would ever, be asked of anyone in the history of the world.

At his moment of decision in the Garden of Gethsemane Jesus knew that he faced the prospect of an agonising death nailed to a cross. Yet this was not what made his obedience unique, for countless others have suffered similarly horrible deaths. No, terrible as this was, Jesus faced something far more terrible still: to have the all sins of the world piled upon him – as if it were he who had thought and said and done all of these things – and so to lose the intimacy that he had enjoyed with his Father from everlasting to everlasting.

This was no easy thing, even for the Son of God. As Luke tells us, "Being in anguish he prayed more earnestly, and his sweat was like drops of blood falling to the ground."[13] And it was at this point, when his Father was asking him to make the ultimate sacrifice, that Jesus demonstrated his ultimate obedience: "Father, if you are willing, take this cup from me; yet not my will, but yours be done."[14]

Could it be that even Jesus had to be brought to this level

*As a Child*

of obedience? That if the cross had come earlier in his life and ministry he might at that time have been unable to go through with it? For we must always remember that, although fully God, Jesus was also fully human. He came as a baby and he needed to grow. He grew in strength[15] and he grew in wisdom,[16] so why should he not also grow in obedience? And if Jesus grew into obedience to what God was calling him to do, then so can we.

Obedience requires the setting aside of self, and of self-determination – of the freedom to feel that we can have what we want and do what we want whenever we want. It requires, in a word, humility. "Your attitude should be the same as that as Jesus Christ: who ... being found in appearance as a man ... humbled himself by becoming obedient to death – even death on a cross!"[17]

The humility of Christ was the humility of a little child, for he "made himself nothing"[18], as a little child is "nothing". And the obedience of Christ was the obedience of a little child, for it came not from submission to authority like a slave with his master, but rather from the childlike relationship with his heavenly Father; for he did what he saw his Father doing.[19] This was not primarily obedience to instruction and command, but rather a heart-felt desire to join his Father in his work. And as it was for Christ, so should it be for us.

# Discipline

Endure hardship as **discipline**; God is treating you as his children. For what children are not disciplined by their father?[1]

As I write this, England has been shocked by several days of rioting and looting that have broken out across London and elsewhere. In my home town, on the outskirts of London, an 11 year old boy has been charged with taking part in the looting of a department store.

In the inevitable debate and discussion that has followed there have been many different opinions about the social and economic causes of the riots, and of the action that needs to be taken to deal with the rioters and to prevent it happening again in the future. One common cry, however, has been the need for parents to provide greater discipline for their children.

There is a well known saying, "Spare the rod and spoil the child" – in other words, if you fail to discipline your child then he will fail to develop a good character and fail to grow into the person that he could have become. In the Bible the book of Proverbs contains similar instruction: "He who spares the rod hates his son, but he who loves him is careful to discipline him,"[2] "Do not withhold discipline from a child; if you punish him with the rod, he will not die."[3] The idea is

## As a Child

"short term pain for long term gain."

It is arguable that, in the past, children suffered from too much discipline, constrained and restrained in their natural childlike exuberance, and subject to unnecessary and inappropriate levels of physical and emotional punishment from parents, teachers, and even the law of the land. In recent years, however, it could be said that the pendulum has swung the other way. Our desire for our children to feel loved and valued, and our fear of them being abused, has arguably caused us to withhold discipline, or else so soften its blow that it ceases to be effective.

But if we find it hard to know how best to discipline our children and young people, then how much harder do we find it to know how it is that God disciplines us? Some see him as an austere father or strict headmaster or severe judge, and consider every hardship and misfortune as some form of discipline or punishment. Others know him to be a loving and merciful God, know that Jesus has taken the punishment for all our sin and wrong-doing, and so never expect the Father's discipline and never recognise it when it comes.

It is neither right nor healthy to assume that all – or, indeed, most – of the hardships that we experience are the result of God disciplining us for some wrong-doing. On the other hand, we do not want to miss and ignore those times when he does discipline and correct us. As the writer of the book of Hebrews counsels, "Do not make light of the Lord's discipline, and do not lose heart when he rebukes you, because the Lord disciplines those he loves, and he punishes everyone he accepts as a son."[4] We need somehow to find the right balance between these two extremes: between missing what is the Lord's discipline and agonising about what isn't.

Quite understandably, children feel very aggrieved if they

## Discipline

are disciplined when they believe that they have done nothing wrong. Because of this, a good parent (or teacher) will never discipline a child without making it clear to him why they are doing so. If this is the case with imperfect human parents, then how much more so with our perfect heavenly Father. But let's be honest, most of us are usually only too well aware when we have "sinned and fallen short of the glory of God."[5] Standing before him we can not help but feel like disobedient children before their parents. We may make excuses and try to shift the blame, but deep down we know when we are in the wrong. This being the case, if we genuinely struggle to identify why God might be disciplining us, and he appears to be staying resolutely silent on the subject, then it is unlikely that we should see our hardship as his discipline.

The writer of the book of Hebrews reminds us that "our fathers disciplined us for *a little while* as they thought best";[6] and Paul, writing to the church in Corinth says to them, "I see that my letter hurt you, but only for *a little while* ..."[7] (italics mine). To cause someone — and especially a child — to suffer for an extended period is not discipline, its abuse; and it goes without saying that our heavenly Father is not an abusive parent. God will discipline us for a little while only; anything more — any hardship that drags on and on — is unlikely to be sent by him.

Of course, being disciplined is not a pleasant experience — and it isn't meant to be. But the pain is not the purpose of discipline — is not an end it itself. Rather, as the writer of Hebrews recognises, it is there to produce "a harvest of righteousness and peace for those who have been trained by it."[8] Writing to the church in Corinth Paul distinguishes between the "Godly sorrow" that results from the Father's discipline and the "worldly sorrow" that has its roots else-

## As a Child

where: "Godly sorrow brings repentance that leads to salvation and leaves no regret, but worldly sorrow brings death."[9] If we feel condemned and lose heart then we are not receiving God's discipline, for this will always have a positive outcome, and ultimately leave us feeling encouraged and uplifted. It is given to help us on our walk with him, not to hold us back and drag us down.

As parents, there are a number of ways in which we can discipline our children. We can "tell them off", admonishing and reprimanding, speaking to them in strong words, raising our voice, perhaps even shouting. We can send them to their room or, with younger children, tell them to "sit on the bottom stair". We can withdraw a privilege or prevent them from doing something they want to do: watch the television, play on the computer, see a friend. Teenage children may be "grounded," and not allowed to go out and "do their own thing". Though contentious, some parents may consider it appropriate to use limited physical pain and smack their children when they are naughty.

In all of these ways, God our heavenly Father can discipline us, his children. He can speak words of admonishment and rebuke: through the Bible, through the "inner voice" of his Holy Spirit, and through the words of others. He can send us from his presence and from the companionship of others, compelling us to take some "time out" on our own, and to consider our behaviour. He can step in and prevent us from doing something that we want to do, frustrating the plans we make for ourselves. And perhaps there are even times when some form of limited pain and suffering is the only way he can get through to us.

Now I well appreciate how hard it can be to discern the

*Discipline*

Father's discipline in amongst the inevitable difficulties of everyday life. And I am aware also that some might see God's punishment in serious illness or other personal tragedy — which is not what I mean at all. I would simply suggest that if things begin to go less well for us, if we feel that there has been a lessening of God's presence, of his blessing, of this hand upon our lives, then this may be his discipline. When such situations arise, therefore, we should not pass them off without a thought. Rather, we should have our eyes and ears and hearts and minds open to receive any correction that God might have for us, that we might be trained by it and brought to repentance. Remember, if it is of God then we will know in our heart-of-hearts what it is we have done wrong, the discipline will last "only for a little while", and, when acted upon, will leave us feeling better able to continue our journey of faith.

"We have all had human fathers who disciplined us and we respected them for it. How much more should we submit to the Father of our spirits and live!"[10]

# Pray

"This, then, is how you should **pray**: 'Our Father in heaven ...'"[1]

Here, of course, are the opening words of the most famous prayer in Christendom. The Lord's Prayer must have been prayed by almost every believer ever since Jesus gave it to us in response to his disciples' request, "Lord, teach us to pray." But despite its familiarity (dare I say, over-familiarity) there is, I think, an important aspect of the prayer that we can easily overlook: that in praying to God as our Father we are necessarily praying to him as his children. Hence, when we come to God in prayer, we are to do so just like a child coming to her father, wanting to talk with him and ask something of him.

We are now so familiar with The Lord's Prayer that it is almost impossible for us to think of it being any other way. But Jesus' use of such language shocked and appalled the religious authorities of the day – and indeed, would have been hardly less shocking to any God-fearing Jew. They knew that God was to be approached as a mighty king – indeed, as the Almighty King – with fear and trembling and reverence and awe. Yet here was Jesus telling his disciples to approach God as a child approaches his father; yes, with

*As a Child*

respect, but also with confidence and joy, and the certainty of his love and care and concern.

Jesus used the same imagery in his teaching elsewhere on prayer: "If you then, though you are evil, know how to give good gifts to your children, how much more will your Father in heaven give good gifts to those who ask him."[2] To pray like a child means to ask like a child: to come to our heavenly Father and simply ask him for what we want. This, however, is something that some of us are rather reluctant to do. We feel that it is not quite right somehow for us to come to God and just reel off a litany of requests; we believe that prayer should be so much more than this. And yes, prayer should be so much more than this. But, if we are not careful, we can make prayer so much less than this, as in our desire to pray with supposed maturity we end up neglecting the very thing that Jesus tells us to do – which is to ask for what we want.

Such an approach also has the dubious "benefit" that the less we ask of God, the less we will be disappointed when our prayers seem to go unanswered; in this way, not praying becomes a simple and rather effective protection mechanism. But, of course, the flip-side is that the less we ask of God, the less we will rejoice and be encouraged when our prayers are answered. As James warns us, "You do not have because you do not ask God."[3] Little children are always ready to ask their parents for help and provision; there's no hesitation or worrying about whether it is "right" that they do so. In the intimacy and security of the parent-child relationship, to ask is the most natural thing in the world. And in the same way we, like little children, are to be always ready to turn to our heavenly Father and ask of him in prayer.

I was pondering such an approach to prayer whilst on holiday

## Pray

with my family. One day we went on a cycle ride and, not having a "proper" paper map of the area, we took our sat-nav with us. Unfortunately, on setting out on our return journey we discovered that we'd somehow lost the sat-nav – and, despite much searching, it was nowhere to be found. It occurred to me that perhaps I should try putting in to practice what I "preached"; that I should do what a little child would do when he lost something, and ask my heavenly Father to help me find it. You might perhaps be unsurprised to learn that the sat-nav still didn't turn up, and we cycled back without it (fortunately the route was fairly straightforward). But this is how it is with prayer: it is not a spell or incantation that we have simply to recite in order magically to get what we want. I have absolutely no idea how or why prayer "works" or "doesn't work" (as we might see it) but I do know that God tells us to keep on asking nonetheless.

Indeed, such persistence is another very childlike quality that God tells us we need to have. Every parent will have experienced this with their own children: when they really want something, they just will not take "no" for an answer!

My daughter loves animals, and she set her heart on having a pet. Now my wife and I are full of appreciation for animals in the wild; we just don't want any in the home, and so have always steadfastly resisted her pleas (except for a brief period when we "generously" allowed her to have a couple of goldfish). Yet, despite this, our daughter was not to be deterred. She kept asking us if she could please have a hamster for her birthday, and somehow we ended up succumbing to her request. Just how did this happen?

Jesus encourages just such childlike persistence in the parable of the persistent widow.[4] (Notably, there are many

## As a Child

places in the Bible where widows and children are spoken of in the same breath, both lacking power and influence, often vulnerable and down-trodden.) Luke makes the point that Jesus told his disciples this parable in order "to show them that they should always pray and not give up." The widow was unable to obtain the justice that she desired because the judge had absolutely no concern for her or the righteousness of her cause. But not to be put off she kept on and on asking; and eventually he became so fed up with her constant badgering that he gave her what she wanted just to shut her up and get her off his back. The point of the parable is not that God is like that unjust judge, but rather that if he "who neither feared God nor cared about men" eventually responded to the widow's persistence, how much more should we persist in praying to our loving heavenly Father, who delights to give good things to his children.

And this is why our daughter received a hamster for her birthday: not because she wore us down with her asking, but rather because her persistence showed us just how much she desired a pet, and we realised that we wanted to give her the joy and happiness it would bring.

So does this mean that God needs to see our persistence in prayer in order to prove the strength of our desire for what we ask? To be honest, I don't know. I suspect that this may at times be one part of the mystery that is prayer, but it is by no means as simple and straightforward as that. All I do know is that God tells us to ask like little children, and to keep asking like little children, and to trust him, as our loving heavenly Father, to answer.

Such persistence does not mean, however, that we have to use long, wordy prayers that go on and on. Indeed, Jesus specifically tells us not to "keep on babbling," thinking that

*Pray*

we will be heard because of our many words, "for your Father knows what you need before you ask him."[5] It is not long prayers but frequent prayers that our Father seeks; not to pray and forget, but to pray and to pray; to keep the object of our prayers close to our heart and to the forefront of our mind, that we might keep turning to him and asking him to grant us those things that we seek.

Incidentally, when we returned from our cycle ride, the missing sat-nav turned up in one of the bags that we'd taken with us and had searched so thoroughly earlier. Coincidence? Quite possibly. All I can say for certain is that I had asked God to help me find it, and now here it was. You might baulk at the idea of a God who apparently locates lost sat-navs when so many much more important prayers – about sickness and disease, poverty and famine, conflict and war – seemingly go unanswered. And in many ways I would share such sentiments; indeed, I hesitated over whether I should mention the episode at all. Yet this is the typical concern of an adult; little children are not bothered about whether what they ask for is "important" or "significant" enough. They simply ask out of the reality of their felt needs and desires, and are thankful when their requests are answered.

This is not to say, of course, that we should be childish in our prayers, asking for anything and everything that we want; as James warns us, if we seek simply to satisfy our own selfish desires, then we should not expect to receive the things for which we ask.[6] Nonetheless, it must surely be better to pray for many things, even if some of them are "wrong", than to pray for too little. And so we are to ask with a childlike confidence, praying "on all occasions with all kinds of prayers and requests,"[7] being thankful and encouraged by all answered prayer, no matter how seemingly trivial. And we are to keep on asking for those more important things that we have yet to receive, having a childlike persistence born out of a heart-felt desire for God's kingdom to come more and more in our lives, in the Church and in the world.

# Praise

"From the lips of children and infants you have ordained **praise**."[1]

I belong to a church in which the children are encouraged to come to the front to sing and dance, and wave flags and streamers during the times of praise and worship. Now doubtless it is a good thing that they are able to take part in the services in this way, rather than having to sit quietly bored whilst we adults sing in our serried ranks. It is good that they can feel welcome in church, able to be themselves rather than having to be on their best behaviour. But one has to ask, is what they're doing really praise? Do the children truly understand what they are singing or appreciate the One to whom their "praise" is directed? Isn't it just that they enjoy this time for its own sake? Would it make any difference if they were singing and dancing to regular pop songs? Quite frankly, is it really any different to being at a party or disco (if not quite so much fun)?

A very similar question might be asked of the children whom we find with Jesus in the temple courts after his triumphal entry into Jerusalem, shouting "Hosanna to the Son of David!"[2] Did they really know what they were saying? Did they have any idea of who Jesus was, or what he

## As a Child

had come to fulfil? Or were they simply joining in the fun, caught up in the excitement of the moment, parroting the praise of the crowd that had welcomed Jesus as he came riding on a donkey?[3]

Certainly the chief priests and teachers of the law thought so: "Do you hear what these children are saying?" they asked him.[4] Of course, they didn't even accept the truth of the acclamation – that Jesus was the Son of David, the Messiah who was to come – but it was undoubtedly doubly disturbing for them to hear his praises sung by naive, impressionable children.

Jesus' reply is telling: "Have you never read, 'From the lips of children and infants you have ordained praise'?" He is completely unconcerned by the fact that the children might not understand just who he is, might not understand the meaning of what they are shouting. This matters not at all; Jesus welcomes their praise. Indeed, more than simply welcomes, for he declares that God has specifically chosen children and infants to praise him. The praise of children is indeed true praise.

The purpose of praise is to glorify God; the focus of our praise is Jesus himself. This might seem an unnecessarily obvious thing to say, and yet it is very easy slip into seeing praise from our point of view rather than God's, to allow the focus to drift away from God and onto ourselves. And this can happen from the seemingly best of intentions. We want to be sure that our praise and worship is more than just words – we want it to be meaningful and heartfelt; we want to "engage with God" and "touch his heart." But the unintended consequence can be that we judge the success of our praise by how we ourselves feel. Did we feel in a "good place" with God? Did we sense something of his presence? Did our praise "rise to the heavens" or did it seem to bounce back to us off the ceiling?

But ultimately none of this much matters, because praise is not about us, it is about God. The purpose of praise is to glorify God – and if he is glorified then the praise is acceptable to him. Children may understand little of what they are saying or of the One to whom they direct their praise, but in their "ignorance" and innocence they give Jesus the honour that is due his name. God's praise in being sung, and so he is being praised. This is in stark contrast to the religious leaders of Jesus' day, who for all their learning were unwilling to do the same (and indeed, it could be argued that their learning was actually an obstacle to them recognising Jesus for who he is).

If we still think that our understanding and awareness of God is an important factor in the reality of our praise, then we need only consider the fact that God does not need us to praise him. He could call forth praise from the very fabric of our buildings: from the bricks and stones, the roof and floor, the windows and doors. For as Jesus replied to the Pharisees when they told him to rebuke his disciples for praising God: "If they keep quiet, the stones will cry out."[5]

Praise could continue on quite happily without us, just as it has done from the very dawn of Creation. As the Psalmist writes, "The heavens declare the glory of God; the skies proclaim the work of his hands. Day after day they pour forth speech; night after night they display knowledge."[6]

We tend to take this to mean that the peoples of the world can learn of God and his glory through the splendours of the natural world; and of course this is right. But first and

## As a Child

foremost the heavens declare the glory of God not to us, but to the One who created all things. His praise has been ringing out across the vast expanse of the Universe ever since he spoke it into being.

In another psalm the call to praise is directed specifically at Creation itself: angels and heavenly hosts; sun, moon and stars; sea creatures and ocean depths; lightning and hail; snow, clouds and winds; mountains and hills; fruit trees and cedars; wild animals and cattle; small creatures and flying birds; kings, princes and rulers; young men and maidens; old men and children. "Let them praise the name of the LORD, for his name alone is exalted, his splendour is above the earth and the heavens".[7]

Animals and inanimate objects offering praise to God? How can this be? They certainly do not understand what it is they are doing; they can not consciously and deliberately offer praise. And yet, by simply being the things that God created them to be, and doing the things God created them to do, praise flows naturally from them. If Creation can naturally and unconsciously praise God then so can little children, and so can we.

Now please understand, I am in no way advocating the mindless singing of theologically suspect songs. When the children in the temple courts shouted "Hosanna to the Son of David" they might not have understood the truth of what they were saying, but it was the truth nonetheless. We praise God for who he is, not for who he is not.

Jesus told the Samaritan woman, "The true worshippers will worship the Father in spirit and truth, for they are the kind of worshippers the Father seeks."[8] But the word "truth" means so much more than doctrinally correct. Jesus came "full of grace and truth"[9] to be "the way and the truth and the life"[10]. Everything that he said, everything that he did, everything that he was demonstrated the way that things are meant to be; this is the meaning of "truth" in its fullest sense. And so, if we are to praise God "in spirit and in truth" then we must do so with the right attitude and without pretence; for God does not look at the outward appearance, he looks at the heart.[11] Indeed, it is not bad doctrine in song that causes God to reject our praise, but rather a lack of "truth" in our lives.

The words of the prophet Amos should serve as a warning to us whenever we are tempted to become too self-satisfied and self-absorbed with our praise: "I hate, I despise your religious feasts; I cannot stand your assemblies ... Away with the noise of your songs! I will not listen to the music of your harps. But let justice roll on like a river, righteousness like a never-failing stream!"[12]

Praise and worship that is not offered "in spirit and in truth" will not be acceptable to God, regardless of how theologically sound it might be; whilst, conversely, the occasional doctrinal digression is unlikely to be cause for too much concern. The great "I AM" does not need us to remind him who he is; he knows that full well.

Indeed, it is perhaps we ourselves who suffer most from singing songs containing poor theology. These can reinforce in us misapprehensions of just who God is and what he does, and this is turn can affect how we relate to God and how we seek to live our lives in him. This being the case, I can imagine Jesus graciously accepting such praise, whilst at the same time drawing alongside us and gently seeking to lead us into more of his truth.

## As a Child

In his essay "First and Second Things" the writer C S Lewis considers the importance of priorities, of ensuring that we put first things first. We can not obtain "second things", Lewis says, by seeking them for their own sakes, by making these the objects of our desire. Rather, we must value and pursue the "first things" – the greater things – and then these "second things" will follow.

This principle holds true in many different areas of our life and faith, and it certainly holds true with our praise. If we seek after "reality" then we risk missing both the reality we seek and, more importantly, the true praise that God desires. But if we seek simply to offer our praise to God, then he will truly be praised, and through such praise he may graciously grant us a glimpse of the reality that we desire.

The praise of little children reminds us that true praise is all about God. It also reminds us that it comes from those who are truest to themselves, who are closest to being the people that God created them to be. So let us become like little children, and learn from them, and join with them in the joy of instinctive, spontaneous, unselfconscious praise.

# Hinder

"Let the little children come to me, and do not **hinder** them, for the kingdom of heaven belongs to such as these."[1]

The scene for this exchange was, according to Mark's account, a house in Capernaum. Jesus had been with his disciples in Judea, on the other side of the Jordan river, healing and teaching the large crowds that flocked to see him. It had doubtless been a long and tiring day, and now his disciples just wanted a bit of peace and quiet and rest and relaxation after the day's exertions. They also wanted to quiz Jesus about the answer that he'd given to some Pharisees who'd come to test him with a question about divorce. All told, they doubtless just wanted to be left alone and have a little time to themselves. Instead of which there's a seemingly never-ending stream of people coming to the house, bringing their babies and little children to be touched and prayed for by Jesus. Perhaps the disciples didn't mind too much at first, but after a while they begin to get more and more agitated and irritated, and just want the people and their children to go away and leave them in peace.

It's possible that had the interruption come from someone more "important" they might not have minded so much. If it had been a religious leader or a Roman Centurion or a royal official or a rich young man, it might have been a different matter. Or even if it had been just an "ordinary" person, but coming for healing from some serious affliction – blindness or leprosy or paralysis, say – again, perhaps the disciples might (albeit grudgingly) have allowed their time with Jesus to be disrupted. But babies and little children! Why, they're too young to understand anything about Jesus; they can't appreciate anything of who he is and what he's come to do. Surely Jesus' time would be better spent teaching those who could understand, accept and follow his teaching, and healing those who could then go and tell others of the healing that they've received? These babies and children couldn't do any of that. And as for the noise and disruption! Babies crying, little children screaming and shouting and running and laughing; their parents and carers admonishing those who have got too excited by it all, and calling after those who have disappeared off into the crowd. Oh no, this is the last thing that Jesus needs! And, truth be told, it is the last thing that the disciples need.

And so the disciples take it upon themselves to act like the entourage of a modern-day celebrity, controlling access to Jesus, allowing through only those whom they deem significant enough to see him, and keeping the rest of the people at bay. And Jesus' response to this? Was he grateful for their intervention and pleased that they had tried to protect his peace and quiet and their chance of some "quality time" together? Not a bit of it! Mark tells us that Jesus was "indignant". He was outraged that his disciples should attempt to keep the little children from seeing him, and just as they had rebuked those who had brought the children, so now Jesus rebuked his disciples.

His anger is hardly surprising when one considers that this

## Hinder

all took place not long after the disciples had asked Jesus who was the greatest in the kingdom of heaven, only for him to answer by calling forth a little child. Clearly his disciples had forgotten this already; or perhaps they'd never really understood it in the first place. Perhaps they'd thought that Jesus had been speaking figuratively: that his words applied to those who in some way became like little children, not to the little children themselves? But Jesus' reaction makes clear that this was in no way what he meant. He had called a child to himself not simply as an illustration of what it means to be great in the kingdom of heaven, but because he really wanted the children to come to him.

It is important that we too do not miss the plain meaning of Jesus' message in the rush to apply it to ourselves. Jesus greatly valued the presence of little children, and was eager to spend his time and energy on them, even though they might be too young to understand his teaching, respond to his message and become his disciples. He wasn't looking for any response from them, except perhaps their unselfconscious, heartfelt response to him and to his acceptance and his love.

Sadly, our treatment of children within the church can be rather more like that of the disciples than of Jesus. We don't like the noise and disruption, so we try to keep them quiet and controlled within church, and then parcel them off into their various groups as soon as decently possible, out-of-sight and out-of-mind.

I realise, of course, that many churches are far more child-friendly than the picture I've just painted. The church that I've attended for many years has no problem with children wandering around and making a bit of noise during the service and, as I've mentioned, they are actively encouraged to participate enthusiastically during their time of praise and

## As a Child

worship. I realise also that there is nothing inherently wrong with children leaving the service to go to their own groups; forcing them to sit through the sermon would not be helpful to the children, just as gearing the whole service around the children would not be helpful to the adults. Nonetheless, I can't help but feel that even in child-friendly churches there is still a danger that we might not truly welcome children as Jesus did.

But turning to ourselves, what is it that might hinder the "little child" in each of us coming to Jesus? My guess is that it will be the very same things that caused the disciples to hinder the little children all those years ago – and which, if we're honest, can cause us to hinder little children today. We're comfortable with our "adult" approach to Jesus – often so choreographed and controlled – and we don't want to risk an encounter that might prove to be rather more messy and unpredictable. But perhaps more fundamentally, we undervalue the child within us, and fail to recognise the validity of a childlike approach to Jesus.

Those who come to faith later in life often begin with very little knowledge and understanding of Jesus and how they "should" relate to him. They feel that they don't know how to read the Bible, or to pray, or to behave in church (be it "high" or "low", traditional or contemporary, formal or informal). They look upon those who have been Christians for some years and marvel at their apparent maturity. And so growing in faith becomes a matter of growing in these things – of increasing knowledge and understanding, of daily "quiet times" and Bible reading and prayer, of regular attendance at Sunday services and other meetings, of involvement in the various "ministries" of the church.

## Hinder

These are, of course, all good things, but they do not necessarily indicate a true maturing and deepening of our faith. Nonetheless, we tend to value a faith characterised by such things more highly than the "immature" faith we began with. There are times when we bemoan the fact that we seem to have lost our initial enthusiasm and passion; that "our first love has grown cold". Yet rarely do we consider the possibility that our very focus on these signs of maturity might have caused our faith to become jaded. Little children might not have the knowledge and understanding and maturity of adults, but more often than not they are more "alive", with a greater love of life.

Perhaps the very things that we believe will enable us to come closer to Jesus have actually become a hindrance? Perhaps we need to recover the freedom and joy that comes from approaching him not with the trappings of adulthood, but with the simplicity of a child.

# Blessed

And he took the children in his arms, put his hands on them and **blessed** them.[1]

The word "bless" literally means "speak wellness", and is a declaration of goodness and prosperity upon someone (or something). The original Greek has within it the word *logos*, meaning "speech" or "word" – which is also the title given to Jesus by John at the start of his gospel account. Thus, when Jesus blesses, we have the Word of Life speaking words of life.[2]

However, whilst blessings are given by word, they are also imparted by touch. This is something that we see in the gospel accounts, and also that we feel instinctively. Indeed, we often speak of seeking "the touch of God" upon our lives.

Of course, Jesus did not need physically to touch people in order to bless them with healing and wholeness; he could do so through word alone. Indeed, his words had the power to speak the whole of creation into being.[3] As the faith-filled centurion so rightly recognised and acknowledged when he came before Jesus, "Just say the word, and my servant will be healed."[4]

Nonetheless, more often than not Jesus did not work by word alone, but rather through word and touch together. He

## As a Child

touched those with leprosy and they were healed.[5] He touched the eyes of the blind and they could see.[6] He touched the ears of the deaf and they could hear, the tongue of the mute and they could speak.[7] He took the hand of a dead girl and she was raised to life;[8] he even touched the coffin of a young man, and he too was brought back from the dead.[9]

Indeed, so aware were the people of the power of the touch of Jesus that those who were sick could not wait for his touch, but instead pushed forward to touch him.[10] A woman who had been subject to bleeding for 12 years thought, "If I just touch his clothes, I will be healed" – and she was.[11] Many, indeed, "begged him to let them touch even the edge of his cloak, and all who touched him were healed."[12]

The healing power of touch continued in an arguably even more remarkable way after Jesus' death, resurrection and ascension into heaven; for, as we read in the Acts of the Apostles, "God did extraordinary miracles through Paul, so that even handkerchiefs and aprons that had touched him were taken to the sick, and their illnesses were cured and the evil spirits left them."[13] I'm not at all sure about the theology of this, but there it is in black-and-white. This isn't the healing touch of Jesus, or healing through touching Jesus or even just touching his clothes. This is healing though touching something that has touched someone who has been "touched" by Jesus. Such is the power of the touch of God.

Like those individuals identified in the gospel accounts, we may long for a personal encounter with Jesus, and seek to know his specific touch upon our lives. Or, like the nameless multitude, we may feel that he has little time for us individually, yet stretch out our hands from the crowd, hoping to touch him or his clothes as he passes. Or we may even, like those who touched the handkerchiefs and aprons, content

*Blessed*

ourselves with an experience of Jesus mediated through the ministries of others. And there is no doubt that in all these ways God can meet us and bless us and heal us. Such, as I say, is the power of the touch of God.

And yet for all this, I can't help but wonder if we don't miss out on something of the blessings that God has for us, in the ways in which we come to him and seek his touch upon our lives.

Mark tells us, "People were bringing little children to Jesus to have him touch them."[14] But Jesus wanted to give the children so much more than a simple touch – and so "he took the children in his arms, put his hands on them and blessed them."[15]

I've been looking through some photos of my children when they were babies: cradled in the crook of my arm, resting over my shoulder, lying on my chest. As I write, my eldest is almost 18 and taller than I am, so the times of such closeness are long past. He is much too big – and anyway, would probably be as self-conscious as I would be. Now it's a pat on the back or, in exceptional circumstances, a quick "manly hug".

We never read of Jesus taking an adult in his arms. This might seem an unnecessarily obvious thing to point out; after all, an adult would be too large for Jesus to be able to do this. But this, in itself, is a point worth noting. It is the children that Jesus can take in his arms, the little ones: those who are small or who make themselves small.

The Bible is full of imagery that speaks of a childlike relationship with God, a childlike dependency on God, a childlike intimacy with God:

"For I am the LORD, your God, who takes hold of your

right hand and says to you, 'Do not fear; I will help you.'"[16] As a parent takes the hand of a child who is feeling unsure, insecure, lost and a little afraid, so God takes the hand of the childlike; assuring them of his presence, his protection and his guidance, and so calming their fears.

"As a mother comforts her child, so will I comfort you; and you will be comforted over Jerusalem."[17] God is like a mother whose heart goes out to her children when they are hurting; who picks them up, enfolds them in her arms, comforts them with her kisses, and wipes away every tear from their eyes.[18]

"The eternal God is your refuge, and underneath are the everlasting arms."[19] God is like a father who says to his child, clambering up a tree, going out on a limb, "Don't worry; I'm here; I'll catch you if you fall."

"O Jerusalem, Jerusalem ... how often I have longed to gather your children together, as a hen gathers her chicks under her wings, but you were not willing."[20] God wants to gather us close, to shelter us and protect us, like a hen with her chicks. But are we willing? Are we willing to be like "little chicks" gathered under the loving maternal wing of God?

"He tends his flock like a shepherd: He gathers the lambs in his arms and carries them close to his heart; he gently leads those that have young."[21] Notice that the adult sheep are led, but the young sheep are carried. It is a wonderful thing to be gently led by God, but how much more wonderful to be gathered in his arms and carried close to his heart!

Babies and little children love to be carried, to be cuddled, to be held, to be hugged. It brings them comfort when distressed, security when disturbed, reassurance when afraid. It communicates to them love and care. They do not hide their need for such intimacy. Indeed, they run to their parents in times of trouble and in times of joy. They open wide their arms to embrace and to be embraced. They display great vulnerability and so enjoy great intimacy.

This is not to suggest that we should spend our lives luxuriating in God's embrace. We are not to become like clinging children, hanging on to our heavenly Father and refusing to let go, never "standing on our own two feet", never venturing out into the "big bad world", never risking being hurt by what we find there.

In fact, it is the very security of a strong parent-child relationship with God that enables us to do these things. For if we know that he is there to take our hand when we are feeling unsure, insecure, lost and a little afraid; if we know that he will pick us up, enfold us in his arms, comfort us with kisses and wipe away our tears; if we know that he is there to catch us when we fall; if we know that he will gather us close to shelter and protect us; if we know that he will gather us in his arms and carry us close to his heart; if we know all these things, then we will have confidence to venture out into the world and live the life that he wants us to live.

We don't need to be childlike in order for God to touch us, and heal us and lead us. But often, as adults, this is as close as we allow him to come; close enough to touch, but not close enough to pick us up and enfold us in his arms. This is the limit of our vulnerability and so this is the extent of our intimacy.

Yet God has so much more for us, such greater blessing – if only we would learn to set aside our pride, our self-sufficiency, our self-importance; if only we would acknowledge our insecurities, and fears and failings; if only we would accept God's shelter, and comfort and reassurance; if only we

## *As a Child*

would stop coming to him with adult restraint and reserve, and instead freely run to him like little children.

# Become

"I tell you the truth, unless you change and **become** like little children, you will never enter the kingdom of heaven."[1]

Throughout this book I have sought to show the importance of Jesus' call for us to become like little children; for I truly believe that a childlike approach is key to us living a life of faith within the kingdom of God, and key to us becoming the people and the church that God wants us to be.

Given that you have stayed with me thus far, I trust that you have not completely discounted what I've had to say. Even if you don't agree with it all, I hope that it has at least stirred within you a desire to become more childlike. If so, perhaps the question that you're now asking is, "How? How can I become like a little child now that I am an adult? Surely I cannot simply roll back the years and think and act as if I am young again?"

This question has echoes of another, asked of Jesus by a teacher of the law named Nicodemus after Jesus had told him that he must be "born again": "How can someone be born when they are old? Surely they cannot enter a second time into their mother's womb to be born!"[2]

Jesus answers Nicodemus by telling him that "no one can enter the kingdom of God unless they are born of water and

*As a Child*

the Spirit"[3] – just as no one can enter the kingdom of God unless he changes and becomes like a little child. Being "born again" is the work of God's Holy Spirit, and it is the same Holy Spirit who can change us to become like little children.

To be born again physically would surely be the ultimate fulfilment of what it would mean to become like a little child. So could it be that an over-looked aspect of being "born again" spiritually is the renewal of childlikeness within us?

But whilst it is the Holy Spirit who changes and transforms us, who creates true childlikeness within us, we nonetheless have our part to play in the process. He needs us to cooperate in the work that he seeks to perform in us. It is a partnership between us and God.

So how do we cooperate with God? What can we do? What part can we play?

I suspect that for many the answer that will most readily spring to mind will involve Bible study and meditation, prayer and contemplation, praise and worship, and other such spiritual disciplines. And there is no doubt that these are all ways in which we can draw closer to God, open ourselves up to his Holy Spirit, and allow him to change us, mould and remake us. And yet, as we have seen, whilst good in themselves, our often adult approach to these disciplines can work against the development of childlikeness. They can become part of the problem rather than the solution, reinforcing the adult that we are, rather than the child that God wants us to be.

So what did Jesus say? Well, as we've seen, he didn't say anything religious, anything about such spiritual disciplines. Instead, "He called a little child and had him stand among them."[4]

You want to be great in the kingdom of God? Then be like this child. Not some mythical perfect child of story and imagination, but this real "flesh and blood" child who stands before you now; doubtless the son or daughter of someone in the crowd and known to many of the others there; perhaps even something of a scamp, a bit too lively and spirited, not always as obedient as he might be. This little child is the greatest in the kingdom. Be like this.

We can not compartmentalise our life and faith. We expect and hope and pray that our faith will affect the way we live our lives, but often ignore the fact that the reverse is also true. If we maintain a relentlessly adult approach to life, then little wonder if we find it difficult to adopt a childlike approach to God. But if, on the other hand, we make room to enjoy more childlike moments in our lives, then we will find this childlike attitude spilling over into our approach to our faith and to God. As we become more childlike, so our faith will become more childlike.

When Jesus called a little child to stand before the crowd, in essence he was saying to them, "Look at this child. Listen to this child. Consider this child. Learn from this child. Emulate this child. Become like this child." And this, I believe, is what we need to do: to become more childlike, not primarily in the religious things, but in the everyday things. To rediscover our childhood. To see, once again, the world through a child's eyes.

But how? For many of us our adult ways run deep. The little paths and byways of childhood were abandoned long ago, and now seem lost beneath the brambles and briars of the cares and concerns that have grown up over the years.

Yet these childhood ways are not lost. They are there just waiting to be uncovered and rediscovered. They may be hard to find and follow at first, but the more we use them, the easier it will become. And the best guides to these childhood

## As a Child

paths are, of course, children themselves. They are the ones who know what it is to be a child, and so they are the ones who can show us how we might live like a child once again.

We desire to grow in our faith, to enter into all that God has for us, to become more and more the people that he wants us to be. And all around us we find those who can teach us and encourage us on this journey: our own children (if we are fortunate enough to have them), those of our family and friends, those within our church fellowship and those of the wider community. So let us take every opportunity to see what they are doing and hear what they are saying – to consider their ways and learn from them and seek to emulate them. Better still let us join them in what they are doing – when they allow us to do so!

Children love to explore, love to investigate, love to search out and discover new things. They get enthused and excited about the most fundamental elements of the world around them: textures and colours and shapes. When my children were young, one of our favourite books was *Fuzzy Yellow Ducklings*, a "lift-the-flap" book in which, for example, a bumpy brown triangle transformed into a group of grumpy toads, and a fuzzy yellow circle transformed into the ducklings of the title.

How might it be if we adults were able to see the world in the same way: to truly take-in the "ordinary" and "everyday", and be enthralled by its infinite variety? Many of the greatest artists throughout history have been motivated by this same desire, and have sought to capture and convey something of the beauty and fascination of things that, ordinarily, we allow to pass us by unnoticed. We can learn from such artists and the work they've produced, and be encouraged to look at the world with fresh eyes. But best of all we can learn from the little children, by allowing them to show and tell us what they see, and by catching something of their infectious enthusiasm for all that they daily discover.

And we can allow ourselves to play again. To do something for no other reason than the sheer enjoyment of doing so. Simply to have fun. To "waste time" when we could be doing something "far more important". And to do so wholeheartedly, with all of our attention; not distracted by the incessant nagging of the never ending lists of things that "need" to be done.

Again, it is the little children who can teach us what it means to play. When my children were younger I used to love to help them put together wooden train layouts and construct scenes and buildings with plastic blocks – and then, of course, join them in playing with what we'd made. In this way children can give us the "excuse" to play, and then draw us into their world of imagination.

Now I'll freely acknowledge that most of us will have little desire to play with children's toys when there are no children around; but we can still play in other ways. Arts and crafts, video games and board games, sports and recreation, hobbies and pastimes – all can be "play" if we do them for pure pleasure, just for the fun of it.

And let us be prepared to make "fools" of ourselves having fun: splashing in puddles, kicking up leaves, clambering on trees; building sand-castles, racing the waves, collecting shells and pebbles; flying a kite, playing conkers, hunting for minibeasts; throwing snowballs, building a snowman, going sledging. These are just a few suggestions; the possibilities for such childlike fun are endless – limited only by our imagination and our willingness to set aside our pride and our supposed dignity and maturity. So let us not worry about what

## As a Child

others might think. In the words of the famous Nike slogan, let's "Just Do It!"

Let us be like little children – not in their childishness, but in their childlikeness. Let us seek always to embrace the childlike in the everyday. Let us heed the advice of an advertisement for Clarks shoes from a few years back: "Act your shoe size, not your age"!

Perhaps this all seems too trivial and trite. Where is the spiritual insight and where are the spiritual disciplines to help us grow in childlikeness? But I truly believe that in order to become more childlike, we need to learn to encounter and experience the world as a child once again. And as we do this, so, I believe, will we begin to encounter God as a child and receive his kingdom as a child – as a child, as a child, as a little child.

> O to be a child again! And put off grown up ways.
> To know again the myriad gifts with which you fill my days.
> To know you as my Father, and to know that I'm your son,
> And as a child to trust your ways until my days are done.

# References

**Preface**
[1] Romans 12:2

**Greatest**
[1] Matthew 18:1
[2] 1 Corinthians 12:12–31, esp. vv 22–23
[3] 1 Corinthians 4:16–17
[4] Hebrews 13:7
[5] 1 Corinthians 1:12
[6] Acts 1:6

**Child**
[1] Matthew 18:2
[2] Matthew 16:18
[3] Matthew 17:1–8
[4] John 1:35–42
[5] John 1:47
[6] John 13:29
[7] Acts 1:6

**Childish**
[1] 1 Corinthians 13:11
[2] 1 Corinthians 14:20
[3] Ephesians 4:14–15

*As a Child*

[4] 1 Corinthians 14:12
[5] Matthew 10:16

**Welcomes**
[1] Matthew 18:5
[2] Revelation 3:20
[3] John 14:23
[4] Psalm 8:2 (*King James Version*)
[5] 1 Samuel 16:7
[6] Matthew 2:11a
[7] c.f. Isaiah 55:8

**Change**
[1] Matthew 18:3
[2] Mark 4:19
[3] Galatians 5:19–21

**Humbles**
[1] Matthew 18:4
[2] 1 Peter 5:5; Colossians 3:12
[3] 1 Chronicles 29:11
[4] Philippians 2:5–8
[5] 1 Corinthians 1:26–29
[6] John 12:24
[7] Mark 9:35
[8] Luke 22:26
[9] 1 Corinthians 12:22
[10] Matthew 23:12
[11] Matthew 18:4

*References*

**Enter**
[1] Matthew 18:3
[2] Mark 10:25
[3] Matthew 7:13–14; Luke 13:24
[4] Ephesians 3:18

**Believed**
[1] John 1:12
[2] Mark 10:15
[3] Psalm 34:8
[4] 2 Corinthians 1:21–22

**Revealed**
[1] Matthew 11:25
[2] 1 Peter 1:8–9
[3] J. B. Phillips, *Your God is Too Small*
[4] Revelation 22:13
[5] 1 Kings 8:27
[6] 2 Corinthians 3:6
[7] John 5:39–40

**Receive**
[1] Luke 18:17
[2] Revelation 22:17
[3] 1 Timothy 6:9
[4] Psalm 42:1
[5] Psalm 63:1
[6] Isaiah 26:8
[7] 1 Corinthians 14:1

*As a Child*

   [8] Matthew 7:11
   [9] John 10:10

**Belongs**
   [1] Matthew 19:14
   [2] Ephesians 2:19
   [3] John 14:2–3
   [4] Galatians 4:4–5
   [5] John 14:23
   [6] Luke 17:21
   [7] Romans 8:32
   [8] Matthew 25:14–30
   [9] Luke 9:24

**Called**
   [1] Luke 18:16
   [2] Mark 7:14
   [3] Matthew 20:32–34; Luke 13:12–13
   [4] John 11:43
   [5] Matthew 4:18–22
   [6] Luke 9:1–2
   [7] Matthew 19:14
   [8] Acts 4:13
   [9] Matthew 18:2
   [10] Romans 1:6
   [11] 1 Corinthians 1:9
   [12] Romans 8:28–30
   [13] 2 Timothy 1:9
   [14] 1 Peter 2:21
   [15] 1 Peter 3:9

*References*

[16] Colossians 3:15
[17] Galatians 5:13
[18] Ephesians 1:18
[19] 1 Timothy 6:12
[20] Philippians 3:14
[21] 1 Peter 2:9
[22] 2 Thessalonians 2:14

**Obedient**

[1] 1 Peter 1:14
[2] Proverbs 22:6
[3] Ephesians 6:5–6
[4] Romans 12:2
[5] Deuteronomy 30:11,14
[6] Isaiah 30:21
[7] John 10:10
[8] Romans 6:1–2
[9] Alternative Confession A, Order for Holy Communion Rite A, *The Alternative Service Book 1980*
[10] Jonah 1:2–3
[11] Hebrews 5:8
[12] Hebrews 4:15
[13] Luke 22:44
[14] Luke 22:42
[15] Luke 2:40
[16] Luke 2:52
[17] Philippians 2:5,8
[18] Philippians 2:7
[19] John 5:19

*As a Child*

**Discipline**
[1] Hebrews 12:7
[2] Proverbs 13:24
[3] Proverbs 23:13
[4] Hebrews 12:5–6
[5] Romans 3:23
[6] Hebrews 12:10
[7] 2 Corinthians 7:8
[8] Hebrews 12:11
[9] 2 Corinthians 7:10
[10] Hebrews 12:9

**Pray**
[1] Matthew 6:9
[2] Matthew 7:11
[3] James 4:2b
[4] Luke 18:1–8
[5] Matthew 6:7–8
[6] James 4:3
[7] Ephesians 6:18

**Praise**
[1] Matthew 21:16
[2] Matthew 21:15
[3] Matthew 21:8–9
[4] Matthew 21:16
[5] Luke 19:40
[6] Psalm 19:1–2
[7] Psalm 148

*References*

[8] John 4:23
[9] John 1:14
[10] John 14:6
[11] 1 Samuel 16:7
[12] Amos 5:21,23–24

**Hinder**
[1] Matthew 19:14

**Blessed**
[1] Mark 10:16
[2] c.f. John 1:1–4
[3] Genesis 1:3; Colossians 1:16
[4] Matthew 8:8
[5] Mark 1:40–42
[6] Matthew 20:30–34
[7] Mark 7:32–35
[8] Mark 5:38–41
[9] Luke 7:12–15
[10] Mark 3:10
[11] Mark 5:25-29
[12] Mark 6:56
[13] Acts 19:11–12
[14] Mark 10:13
[15] Mark 10:16
[16] Isaiah 41:13
[17] Isaiah 66:13
[18] Revelation 7:17
[19] Deuteronomy 33:27a
[20] Matthew 23:37

*As a Child*

[21] Isaiah 40:11

**Become**
[1] Matthew 18:3
[2] John 3:4
[3] John 3:5
[4] Matthew 18:2